AF269488

BEACHES
of Newfoundland

Library and Archives Canada Cataloguing in Publication

Title: Beaches of Newfoundland / Carla Smith Krachun.

Names: Smith Krachun, Carla, author.

Description: Includes bibliographical references and index.

Identifiers: Canadiana 20230163769 | ISBN 9781989417652 (softcover)

Subjects: LCSH: Beaches—Newfoundland and Labrador—Guidebooks. | LCSH: Recreation areas—Newfoundland and Labrador—Guidebooks. | LCSH: Outdoor recreation—Newfoundland and Labrador—Guidebooks. |

LCSH: Newfoundland and Labrador—Guidebooks. | LCGFT: Guidebooks.

Classification: LCC GV191.46.N6 S65 2023 | DDC 796.5/309718—dc23

Published by Boulder Books
Portugal Cove-St. Philip's, Newfoundland and Labrador
www.boulderbooks.ca

Cover photo: Carla Smith Krachun (Cape Ray Beach)
Design and layout: Tanya Montini
Editor: Stephanie Porter
Copy editor: Iona Bulgin

Printed in India

We acknowledge the financial support of the Government of Newfoundland and Labrador through the Department of Tourism, Culture, Arts and Recreation.

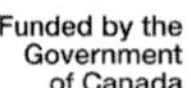

C A R L A   S M I T H   K R A C H U N

BEACHES
of Newfoundland

BOULDER
BOOKS

Contents

Introduction

The familiar image of a Newfoundland beach is a windswept, craggy cove shrouded in fog, stunted trees clinging to cliff faces, and waves lashing at rocks. Such scenes are, indeed, common on the island, but there is another side to Newfoundland beaches. In almost every corner of the island, expansive stretches of soft sand and grass-covered dunes can also be found. In writing this guide, my goal was to help people discover and enjoy the many and varied beaches that Newfoundland has to offer, from jagged coves to sandy expanses, and all the types in between.

This book was not intended to be a complete list of every beach, which would be a monumental task on an island with 10,000 kilometres of coastline. Instead, a healthy sampling of the lesser-known beaches are included with the widely known ones. I hope that everyone—even the most seasoned beachgoer—will find new beaches to explore in this collection.

One of the main criteria used in deciding which beaches to include was their ease of access. Beaches were included if they could be reached by automobile or on foot via reasonably well-maintained roads and hiking trails. Beaches that were accessible only by boat were excluded, except for those on Bell Island and Fogo Island, which are served by large ferries. One of the consequences of excluding difficult-to-reach beaches is that some sections of the coastline, such as the isolated areas along the south coast, are underrepresented. Other areas, such as the heavily populated Avalon Peninsula, have many entries, because roads and walking paths within and between communities have made much of the coastline readily accessible.

Although this book covers only the island portion of the province, Labrador also has many magnificent beaches. Some of them, including the sandy beaches at L'Anse au Claire, Forteau, L'Anse au Loup, and Pinware River Provincial Park, are within an hour's drive of the Labrador ferry dock at Blanc Sablon. Others are far off the beaten track. A boat is required to visit the remote and untouched Wonderstrands north of Cartwright, two adjacent sandy beaches that together total more than 40 kilometres in length. Covering Labrador's beaches was beyond the scope of this project, but the Big Land has its share of natural treasures.

USING THIS GUIDE

One of the most enjoyable aspects of working on this guide was visiting and photographing the beaches I knew and loved while also discovering beaches previously unknown to me. This guide is intended to encourage readers to visit and enjoy these beaches, and to make it as easy as possible to do so. To this end, each entry contains the following information:

Regions and Beach/Place Names

The island is divided into four major regions—Western, Central, Eastern, and Avalon—with the appropriate region displayed at the bottom of the page. Regions are colour-coded for quick identification. Each major region is further divided into sub-regions based on geography, settlement patterns, and highway access points. Sub-regions are displayed at the top of the page, just above the Beach/Place name.

In most cases, the spelling of names is the official spelling listed in the Canadian Geographical Names Database (CGNDB) at the time this guide was published. Places not in the database are spelled according to local convention. When a place is listed in

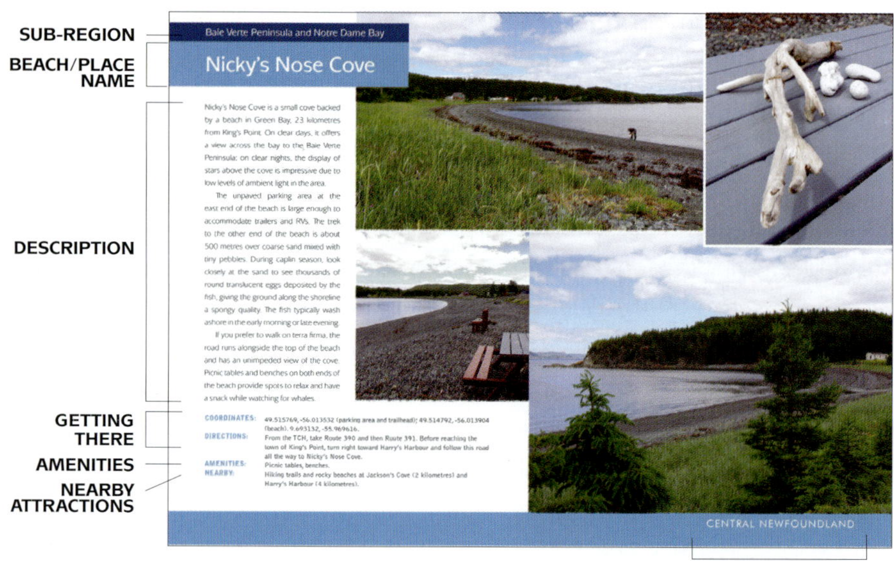

the database under one name but is widely known by another name, the widely known name is used and the official name noted. Alternative unofficial but commonly known names are also sometimes noted.

Beach Description

The description provides details on location, landscape features, infrastructure, historical significance, and any other information that may be of use and interest to readers.

Getting There

Driving directions are given to the beach or, when a hike is required, to the trailhead. Most directions begin with the route number from the Trans-Canada Highway (TCH). When multiple possible routes from the TCH exist, directions are given from the nearest well-known community. Distances are approximate.

Coordinates are also provided as another navigational tool. For accurate results, the coordinates should be entered into the Google Maps search bar exactly as they are presented in this guide, including the minus sign. If a hike to the beach is required, coordinates are also provided for the trailhead. In some entries, coordinates for noteworthy nearby beaches are also given.

Amenities

Features such as change rooms, outhouses, bathrooms (i.e., with flush toilets and sinks), picnic tables, food stands, and campsites are listed. If no amenities are available at the beach, "None" is noted, although in many cases bathrooms, stores, restaurants, and other amenities may be found in surrounding communities.

Amenities may vary over time, as infrastructure is added, upgraded, or sometimes dismantled due to wear or damage. Many amenities, even outhouses, are usually open only during the summer tourist season. This period varies across beaches and parks but can be as short as late June to the end of August. Picnic tables and benches are often removed during the winter to avoid loss or damage. If you are visiting beaches during the off-season, plan accordingly.

Nearby Attractions

Beachgoers may be interested in exploring nearby attractions, such as hiking trails, museums, historical sites, and additional beaches. A brief list of suggestions is provided, along with approximate distances to each site from the beach featured in the entry.

Photographs

The photographs included in this guide give readers a sample of what they can expect to find when visiting the beaches. Most were taken in fair weather to maximize visibility and were not manipulated apart from cropping and

minor corrections to brightness, colour, and contrast. Except where credited to an outside contributor, the photographs were taken by the author in 2021 and 2022.

Beaches are extremely changeable. Tides, currents, wind, and waves constantly shift sand, rocks, and other materials. Under normal circumstances, the largest changes occur over months or years, but dramatic changes can also happen suddenly during severe weather events. Beaches that are mostly sandy one day can be covered in rocks the next, dunes can be heavily eroded overnight, and seaweed or marine debris can blanket a beach that was pristine the previous day. The photographs on these pages are, literally, snapshots in time of the beaches as they were on the day(s) they were visited.

CAUTIONS AND REGULATIONS

Beaches in Newfoundland do not, as a rule, have lifeguards. A life preserver is sometimes available on the shoreline for emergencies, but swimming is typically unsupervised. Extreme caution should be exercised, as very cold water, strong currents, and high waves can present significant dangers. Heed signs that warn against swimming in particular areas. Often, safer places to swim can be found nearby, in the barachois created by a beach or in nearby rivers and lakes, although these will also typically be unsupervised. The safest approach is to swim only in daylight and in fine weather, and only when accompanied by another person. Similar caution should be exercised when boating, surfing, kayaking, paddleboarding, snorkeling, diving, and engaging in any other activities in or on the water.

The condition of roads, trails, and infrastructure such as boardwalks, staircases, ropes, benches, ramps, fencing, railings, and viewing platforms can change quickly in coastal environments. Watch for hazards and do not take unnecessary risks. Ultimately, readers are responsible for their own safety and that of any children or pets in their care.

It is equally important to consider the welfare of the wildlife that depend on our beaches for survival. Many of Newfoundland's beaches host a variety of bird species, some of which are threatened or endangered. Vulnerable areas usually have signs explaining how visitors can enjoy the beach while safeguarding the environment, such as by staying on designated trails and keeping pets leashed. Please observe the regulations.

Provincial parks, national parks, and ecological reserves have particularly strict regulations. Except in designated campgrounds and picnic areas, camping and campfires are not permitted. ATVs and other off-road vehicles are also not allowed, nor is removing sand, stones, or other found items from the beach. Even outside of parks and protected areas, visitors are encouraged to engage in these activities in a responsible manner.

WHEN TO VISIT

Not surprisingly, the answer to "When should I visit Newfoundland's beaches?" is, "It depends." If you are looking for fun in the sun, sand, and surf, July and August are your best bet for warm temperatures. In Newfoundland, there are never any guarantees, however, and the weather can change quickly; it's always a good idea to pack a windbreaker or a warm sweater.

Your greatest chance of spotting icebergs is in the late spring, especially from May to early June. Look for them on the north coast of the island as they drift down from Greenland along a route dubbed Iceberg Alley, which stretches from Labrador to the eastern shore of the Avalon Peninsula. Beyond early June, it becomes less likely that you will see icebergs on the eastern side of the island, as increasing temperatures cause them to melt before they make it that far, but the season is extended in the more northern locations. An excellent resource for locating icebergs is the Iceberg Finder website (icebergfinder.com), run by Newfoundland and Labrador Tourism.

If you are hoping to see whales, the world's largest population of humpback whales feeds in Newfoundland waters from about May to September before heading south for the winter. Humpback whales are the most spotted whales in Newfoundland, but 21 other species of whales and dolphins also visit, including the

obvious reasons, the ice-filled bays and snow-covered cliffs of winter and early spring can be striking. If you do visit during these times, be extra cautious, as rocks will be very slippery and overhanging snow accumulations can be extremely dangerous near cliff edges.

GLOSSARY

As some terms used in this guide may be unfamiliar, a brief glossary of terms and their local usage is provided below.

Backshore: The part of the beach that lies above the normal high-tide line.

Bar beach: A bar composed of sand or rocks that extends across the mouth of a river or bay, separating it from the ocean.

largest whales in the world: blue whales and fin whales. A good time to watch for whales is when caplin are washing ashore by the thousands to spawn, as the whales come closer to shore to feed on the small, silver fish. The annual "caplin roll" is unpredictable but usually happens in June or July. Pay attention: the event generates excitement and discussion among local residents, and many head to the beach with buckets and nets to collect the caplin.

For those who simply want to enjoy the scenery at the beach, almost any time of the year will do. While late spring to early fall are the most popular times to visit for

Barachois (also barasway or barrisway): A shallow lagoon formed by a sand or rock bar that separates the lagoon from the ocean.

Bight: A bend or curve in the coastline that creates a large, open bay.

Boil-up: Tea prepared by boiling a kettle over a campfire in the woods or on a beach, sometimes accompanied by a snack.

Caplin (also capelin): Small fish that wash ashore in large numbers in the summer to spawn on the beach. They are collected to be eaten or used as bait or fertilizer. When caplin begin to wash up on the beach, local residents say the caplin are "rolling," and the event is called the annual "caplin roll."

Cobbles (also cobblestones): Rounded stones ranging from 64 to 256 millimetres in diameter, according to the commonly used Udden-Wentworth scale for classifying rock sizes. Cobbles are larger than pebbles and smaller than boulders.

Devil's purse: See mermaid's purse.

Gut: A narrow channel between two bodies of water, such as the small opening at the end of a sandbar separating the ocean from a pond or lagoon.

Marine debris: Fragments of fishing gear and other debris that wash ashore from the ocean, such as pieces of netting, rope, plastic, wood, and floats.

Mermaid's purse: Also called devil's purse, this egg casing protects the developing embryos of sharks and skates. It has the appearance of a hard, rectangular, dark pouch with "horns" at each corner (see page 141).

Pocket beach: A beach in a small cove that has been carved out of the cliffs by erosion. In Newfoundland, most of the sand and rocks on these beaches were once a part of the surrounding cliffs.

Portuguese man-of-war: A marine animal closely related to jellyfish, with a blue or purple balloon-like float and long tentacles. Its sting is rarely deadly to humans but is quite painful. Keep your distance, as they can retain their ability to sting long after being washed ashore.

Sand dollar: A round, flat marine invertebrate related to sea urchins. Living sand dollars are a dark colour; the white sand dollars found on beaches are the bleached skeletal remains of dead organisms.

Shingles: Another word for pebbles, especially when they are more flattened than rounded.

Spit: A stretch of sand or rocks that extends out into the sea—often used synonymously with sandbar.

TCH: The Trans-Canada Highway, which is Route NL-1 in Newfoundland.

Tombolo: A bar of sand or rocks that attaches an island to the main body of land (e.g., see Heart's Ease Beach).

Tuckamore: An evergreen tree that has been stunted and twisted by a harsh coastal climate.

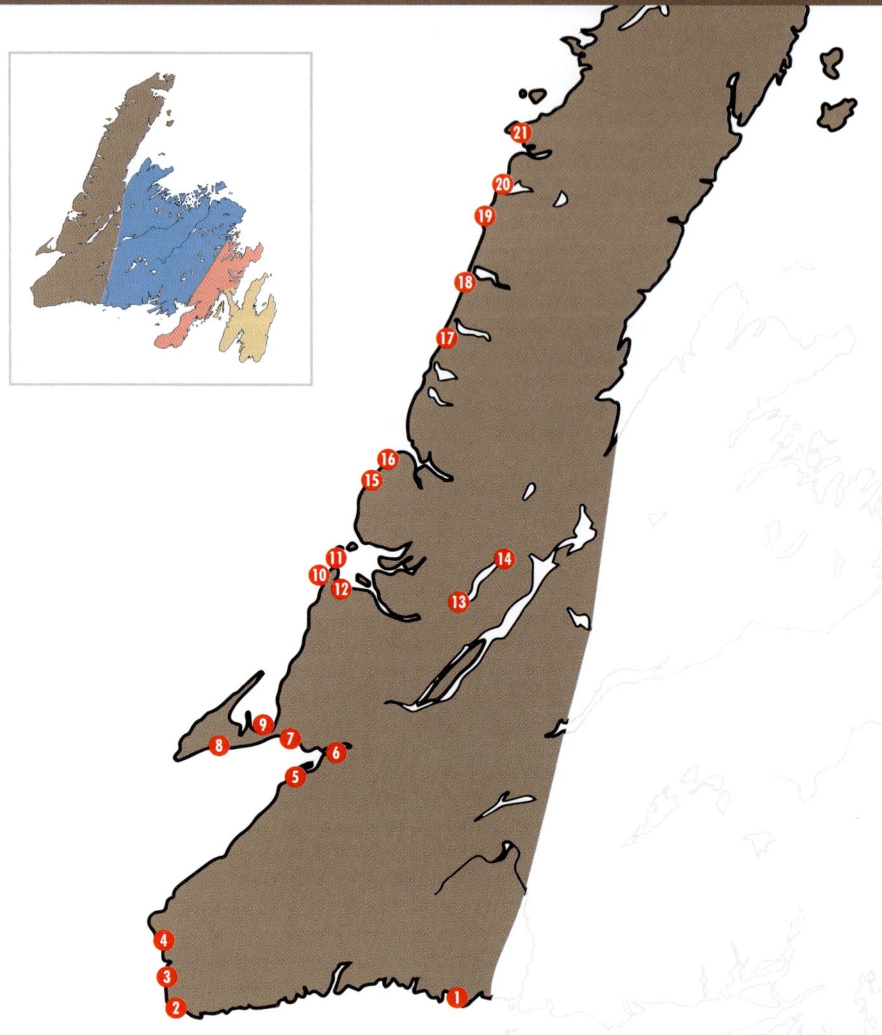

1	Sandbanks Provincial Park	12	Blow Me Down Park
2	Grand Bay West	13	Pasadena Beach
3	Cape Ray Beach	14	Deer Lake Beach
4	Codroy Valley Beach	15	Trout River Beach
5	Flat Bay West	16	Old Man's Cove
6	Black Bank Beach	17	Western Brook Beach
7	Port Harmon Beach	18	Shallow Bay
8	Sheaves Cove	19	Arches Provincial Park
9	Piccadilly Beach	20	Portland Creek
10	Cedar Cove	21	Port au Choix
11	Bottle Cove		

Western Newfoundland

For the purposes of this guide, Western Newfoundland includes the portion of the island stretching westward from Burgeo on the south coast and from Hampden on the north coast. Included in this area are the southwest coast from Channel-Port aux Basques to Port au Port Bay, the Bay of Islands and Humber Valley, Gros Morne National Park, and the Northern Peninsula.

For many Newfoundlanders, the first place that comes to mind when they think about the island's beaches is Sandbanks Provincial Park in Burgeo. With five long, white sandy beaches set in a landscape of barren hills, rocky outcrops, and numerous small lakes and islands, the park is arguably the crown jewel of beaches in Newfoundland. Part of its appeal is just how far it is off the beaten track: 150 kilometres down the long and lonely Caribou Trail (Route 480) through the interior to the south coast. The park lies along a 200-kilometre stretch of coastline punctuated occasionally with tiny outports accessible only by passenger ferry. It's the perfect place to unplug and experience one of the most remote parts of the island.

Farther west, at the extreme southwest tip of the island, is Channel-Port aux Basques. Most people visiting Newfoundland by car arrive here via the Marine Atlantic ferry from Cape Breton. Sandy beaches are a short drive from the ferry terminal, including Grand Bay West Beach that was hit hard by post-tropical storm Fiona in 2022. More sandy beaches are located at Cape Ray and a little farther north in the Codroy Valley.

In and around St. George's Bay are several more beaches, accessed via Routes 403 and 490 off the TCH. A hidden gem in this area is Black Bank Beach with its towering, sand-covered banks, just outside the community of Barachois Brook. Those interested more in stones than sand may want to visit Port Harmon Beach in Stephenville with its pebbles and cobbles in an astounding variety of colours, shapes, and sizes.

The Port au Port Peninsula, bordering the north side of St. George's Bay, is known less for its beaches than for its sheer

coastal cliffs. Many are visible from the French Ancestors Route, the name of the highway that loops around the peninsula, in recognition of the area's strong French heritage. Particularly dramatic coastal vistas can be seen in Boutte du Cap Park at Cape St. George, which also has a monument to the Acadians that settled in the region in the 18th and 19th centuries. Long, narrow beaches lie below many of the cliffs, but do not risk trying to access them. Instead, visit the easily accessible beaches at Sheaves Cove or Piccadilly Head.

North of St. George's Bay, the TCH runs inland to Corner Brook, the third largest city in the province with nearly 20,000 residents. From Corner Brook, Route 450 (Captain Cook's Trail) follows the south shore of Humber Arm in the Bay of Islands for approximately 50 kilometres. With the Blow Me Down Mountains on one side and Humber Arm on the other, the scenery along the route does not disappoint. Many of the islands that earned the Bay of Islands its name are visible, among them Woods Island, Governors Island, and the large mound-shaped Wee Ball in the entrance to the bay. The route ends at Lark Harbour, which boasts three beaches at Cedar Cove, Bottle Cove, and Blow Me Down Provincial Park. Near each beach are hiking trails that will take you up the surrounding hills for wide-open coastal views.

East of Corner Brook, the TCH leads

Northern Peninsula along Route 430 (the Viking Trail). Rated by Lonely Planet in 2022 as one of the seven best road trips in Canada, the route runs first through Gros Morne National Park, a designated UNESCO World Heritage Site. There is much to explore in the park, including over 100 kilometres of hiking tails. Beach lovers will appreciate the chance to camp next to a sandy beach at Shallow Bay, eat seafood in a restaurant overlooking the beach in Trout River, or hike to a beach with volcanic rock formations on the Green Gardens Trail. A day or season pass is required for all Gros Morne sites and facilities. Passes can be purchased throughout the park and surrounding communities, including at the Gros Morne Entrance Kiosk in Wiltondale.

North of Gros Morne Park, the drive along Route 430 offers impressive coastal views. The most well-known attraction is the site of a 1000-year-old Viking settlement at L'Anse aux Meadows, on the northern tip of the peninsula. As you make your way there, pause to see the rock arches at Arches Provincial Park, the archaeology exhibits at Port au Choix, and the rare rocklike "thrombolites" formed by ancient bacteria at Flower's Cove. Although they are not the main attraction, rocky beaches can be found at or near each of these sites.

away from the coast, but two popular swimming beaches lie on the shores of Deer Lake, a long, narrow freshwater lake at the heart of the Humber Valley. The lake drains into the Bay of Islands via the Humber River, which, in the first half of the 20th century, was used to float logs down to the pulp and paper mill in Corner Brook. These days, logs are transported by truck, but on a hot summer day, you may see rafters and tubers floating their way down the river.

At the north end of the lake is the Town of Deer Lake, often referred to as the Gateway to the North. A highway interchange on the edge of town takes you off the TCH and up to the tip of the

1 Sandbanks Provincial Park

At the end of a long, remote highway with no amenities, Sandbanks Provincial Park in Burgeo is undeniably off the beaten path. The reward for those who make the trek is 7 kilometres of sandy beaches in a beautiful and barren landscape. The soft, white sand is unusual for the mostly rugged and rocky south coast. According to Parks Canada, the sand originated from glacial deposits acted upon over millennia by complex wave patterns created by the numerous offshore islands in the area.

Most of the beaches are accessible via a network of hiking trails that loop around the park. To travel counterclockwise around the loop, take the path between campsites 13 and 15, which runs alongside Heron Pond and then out to Western Beach. Stop to beachcomb among the driftwood, or take a picture by Aaron Island, a tiny island attached to the beach by a short tombolo.

From Western Beach, rejoin the loop and hike the path out to Grip Head for a sweeping view of the coastline. Continuing along the loop, side trails lead to more sandy beaches and scenic lookouts. Near Cow House Hill, look for the remains of a 19th-century cemetery with eroded gravestones half buried in the sand. From there, the trail follows the coastline back to the parking area, passing more sandy beaches with opportunities to view sandpipers and piping plovers.

For those who prefer a beach visit without the hike, First Beach is about 200 metres southeast of the parking lot by the park entrance. Firepits and picnic tables are provided, including a wheelchair-accessible table just above the beach. A freshwater pond with an unsupervised swimming area is in the park next to the campground. The park charges a day-use fee.

COORDINATES: 47.607192, -57.644713.

DIRECTIONS: From the TCH, take Route 480 to Burgeo (gas up first as there are no service stations en route). Turn right onto Inspiration Road by Gillett's Motel, then right onto Main Street, which soon becomes Messieurs Road. Follow Park Road to the park entrance.

AMENITIES: Unserviced campsites, picnic tables, firepits, outhouses, and a wheelchair-accessible comfort station with flush toilets, showers, and laundry.

NEARBY: Farley Mowat's House (2 kilometres), Maiden Tea Hill (3 kilometres), Burgeo Ferry to south coast outports (4 kilometres).

WESTERN NEWFOUNDLAND

2 Grand Bay West

Grand Bay West Beach, located on the western edge of Channel-Port aux Basques, is an example of the destructive potential of the ocean. Before September 2022, the beach was a popular destination for locals and visitors wanting to relax on the sand, stroll on the boardwalk, or hike the coastal trail around the point to a second beach.

On September 24, 2022, the beach sustained extensive damage from post-tropical storm Fiona, which took one life and damaged beyond repair more than 100 homes in the area. The 400-metre boardwalk that skirted Grand Bay West Beach was destroyed, as were lookouts along the coastal trail. Other sections of the trail were also heavily damaged or washed away, making them unpassable.

The positive news is that the town council decided to repair and rebuild, using some of the wood salvaged from the original boardwalk. As of 2023, it was still uncertain how long this process would take and what adjustments would need to be made to the original trail design and location.

COORDINATES: 47.582835, -59.184659.

DIRECTIONS: On the TCH, approximately 5 kilometres northwest of Channel-Port aux Basques, a sign directs you to Grand Bay West. Follow this road for 2.7 kilometres to Kyle Lane, then turn right and drive for another 300 metres to the parking area.

AMENITIES: Wheelchair-accessible bathroom and change rooms, picnic tables, chairs, and benches. (These amenities may be temporarily unavailable due to storm damage.)

NEARBY: Railway Heritage Centre (2 kilometres), Scott's Cove Park/Harbour Boardwalk (5 kilometres), Cape Ray Beach (12 kilometres).

WESTERN NEWFOUNDLAND

3 Cape Ray Beach

Cape Ray Beach is a long, sandy barachois beach located in J.T. Cheeseman Provincial Park. Just a 15-minute drive from Port aux Basques, the beach is a perfect place to stop after the long ferry ride across the Cabot Strait from Nova Scotia. To access the beach, follow the unpaved road through the park to the end, about 3.5 kilometres. A day-use fee is required.

A path from the parking area takes you onto the sand, where a bench invites you to sit and enjoy the scenery before dipping your toes in the ocean. Be aware of the strong tidal action at the unsupervised beach; visitors often prefer to swim in the freshwater barachois.

With its grass-covered dunes, Cape Ray Beach makes an excellent nesting ground for the endangered piping plover, which occupies the area from May to August each year. The nests consist of open depressions in the sand, usually on or near the dunes. To avoid disturbing the vulnerable eggs, be sure to keep dogs leashed and walk near the shoreline.

The 2-kilometre Smokey Cape Trail begins in the day-use area of the park and ends at the beach. The trail is named after the spray from the breaking waves, which can look like smoke as you approach the end of the trail.

COORDINATES: 47.624963, -59.270859.

DIRECTIONS: J.T. Cheeseman Park is approximately 13 kilometres northwest of Port aux Basques on the TCH. Drive 3.5 kilometres from the park entrance to reach the parking area adjacent to the beach.

AMENITIES: Wheelchair-accessible outhouse; other amenities in the park include bathrooms, laundry, and showers.

NEARBY: Cape Ray lighthouse and former site of Dorset settlement (6 kilometres), Scott's Cove Park/Harbour Boardwalk (14 kilometres).

WESTERN NEWFOUNDLAND

4 Codroy Valley Beach

Codroy Valley Beach is on a narrow strip of land between Millville and Searston, in Codroy Valley Beach Provincial Park. Also known locally as Millville Beach, the beach runs northwest to southeast for approximately 1.5 kilometres before being cut off by "The Gut," where the Grand Codroy River empties into the Gulf of St. Lawrence. A traffic bridge crosses the gap to a smaller beach at Searston.

A birdwatcher's paradise, the Codroy Valley hosts species that are seldom or never seen in other parts of the province, such as the great blue heron, rose-breasted grosbeak, and ruby-throated hummingbird. On the beach, view a variety of seabirds and shorebirds, including the endangered piping plover, which nests in the area from May to late August. Signs provide instructions on how to avoid disturbing the nests of this very vulnerable species.

To access the beach, park in the large gravel parking lot in the day-use area of the provincial park, to the west of the traffic bridge. Cross the highway and follow the path over the bank to find a long stretch of fine light sand sprinkled with pebbles and driftwood.

Outhouses and a picnic table are available in the parking and day-use area, which has an excellent view of the Grand Codroy River and surrounding Long Range Mountains. Camping is not permitted, but there is a campground in Grand Codroy Park near Doyles, about 10 kilometres east of Searston on Route 406.

COORDINATES: 47.832790, -59.336379.
DIRECTIONS: From the TCH, take Route 406 or 407 toward Searston. Cross the traffic bridge and park across from the beach on Route 407, about 1 kilometre west of Searston.
AMENITIES: Outhouses, picnic table.
NEARBY: Wetlands Trail (8 kilometres), Murray's Beach at Saint Andrew's (9 kilometres), Cape Anguille Lighthouse (11 kilometres), Starlite Trail (16 kilometres).

WESTERN NEWFOUNDLAND

5 Flat Bay West

Flat Bay West is a Mi'kmaw community on the southwest coast of Newfoundland. The beach is on Flat Island, a peninsula that runs roughly parallel to the southern shore of St. George's Bay for more than 10 kilometres, creating a long, narrow bay.

Interesting for its unusual mix of natural elements, the beach has large stones jumbled with fine white sand. High banks loom above the beach near the base of the peninsula but quickly give way to a wide-open space.

Most striking is the difference between the two sides of the peninsula. On the side exposed to the ocean, gnarled tangles of driftwood and crashing waves make the beach feel wild and alive. The sheltered side, inside Flat Bay, is calmer and softer, with wildflowers and grasses covering the low banks.

Farther down the peninsula are forests, meadows, marshes, freshwater ponds, and, near the end, the site of an abandoned community named Sandy Point. A diversity of people resided at Sandy Point, including Mi'kmaq, English, and French. People with connections to the site still visit the area, mostly by ATV because of the distance. A local tour operator, Pirate's Haven Adventures, offers occasional ATV tours.

COORDINATES: 48.395970, -58.622840.
DIRECTIONS: From the TCH, take Route 403 West (Flat Bay Road) and drive for 11.3 kilometres. At the T-junction, turn left toward St. Teresa's to stay on Route 403 (Main Road West) for another 2.7 kilometres. Park in the gravel area above the beach.
AMENITIES: Gazebo, benches, and a firepit overlooking the beach.
NEARBY: Playground, swimming area, and walking trail at Flat Bay Pond Park (4 kilometres).

Photo © Julie Sircom

WESTERN NEWFOUNDLAND

6 Black Bank Beach

Black Bank Beach is just north of the town of Barachois Brook on Route 461. Steep sand-covered banks create a dramatic backdrop for the beach, which stretches for several kilometres along the coast of St. George's Harbour in St. George's Bay.

The sand is beige, not black, and the name likely refers to the thick, dark conifer forest covering the banks. Atop the banks, ATV trails and walking paths through the trees allow you to explore while enjoying the panoramic view. An old, paved road also runs parallel to the beach along the top of the banks, but it is not maintained and some parts are impassable by car.

Although not widely known, the beach is a popular destination for local residents on hot days. Soft sand mixed with pebbles makes for a comfortable place to sit and sunbathe, and cooling off is easy as the water is shallow near the shore. As with all unsupervised beaches, use caution when swimming. There is no designated picnic area, but you may find a washed-up log to sit on among the driftwood that washes up on the beach.

COORDINATES: 48.465041, -58.431971.

DIRECTIONS: From the TCH, take Route 490 for about 4 kilometres and then turn left onto Route 461. The beach access is approximately 1 kilometre down Route 461, just before you enter the town of Barachois Brook. There is no signage, so watch for the paved road into the parking area on the right.

AMENITIES: None.

NEARBY: Cranberry farm off Carter's Road (5 kilometres), freshwater swimming beaches at Barachois Pond Provincial Park (15 kilometres).

WESTERN NEWFOUNDLAND

7 Port Harmon Beach

A year-round ice-free port in the town of Stephenville, Port Harmon is named for the US Air Force Base that operated there from 1941 to 1966. The beach is on a strip of land that separates Port Harmon from St. George's Bay, with passage into the port located at the southeast end of the beach. Tucked inside the passage is the photogenic Little Port Harmon, a small harbour with colourful docks and fishing boats.

To access Port Harmon Beach, head to Massachusetts Drive in Stephenville and park in one of several pull-ins along the road. Benches are provided near most pull-ins, and a pedestrian/bike path runs along the beach for more than 4 kilometres.

As you explore the beach, notice the sheer variety of rocks present, from rounded pebbles to flat shingles to large cobbles, all occurring in a wide range of colours and patterns. Look toward the southeast end of the beach for a view of Indian Head. The 20-metre-high cliff contains exposed anthrosite, an extremely old type of rock also found on the moon.

The opposite (northwest) end of the beach is a popular spot for campers to park RVs and trailers, although no services are offered. Camping is not permitted in the parking pull-ins along Massachusetts Drive.

COORDINATES: 48.519632, -58.547033.
DIRECTIONS: In Stephenville, take Carolina Avenue to Massachusetts Drive and follow this road to the beach. Park in a gravel pull-in along Massachusetts Drive.
AMENITIES: Benches.
NEARBY: Harmon Seaside Links Golf Course (<1 kilometre), Blanche Brook Park (4 kilometres), Ned's Pond Trail (7 kilometres), Joey's Lookout (13 kilometres).

8 Sheaves Cove

As you travel the south side of the Port au Port Peninsula, the small cobble beach at Sheaves Cove can be easy to miss. Watch closely for the signs, and do not be deterred when it seems as though they are leading you down a private driveway—this is the road to the cove.

Park in the gravel area behind the sheds and stroll on the beach with its pretty stones in shades of pink, grey, and gold. A large rock outcrop on the east side of the beach invites climbing, and some visitors even walk along the rock ledge that runs along the cliff face. Caution is advised, however, due to the slickness of the rocks and the unpredictability of the waves. The beach is also a popular launching point for sea kayakers, although high southerly winds can sometimes make this difficult.

Just north of the beach, in a small, lush valley, are the Hidden Falls. The path leading from the parking area to the falls is about

300 metres and well maintained. Watch for birds in the wetlands below the falls. On the west side of the beach, a staircase will take you up to a 0.5-kilometre walking loop with lookouts and benches. Unusual rock deposits are found along the trail.

COORDINATES: 48.520553, -59.056118 (turnoff from Route 460); 48.517397, -59.052916 (beach).

DIRECTIONS: From Stephenville, take Kippens Road (Route 460) heading west out of town toward the Port au Port Peninsula. Follow Front Street for approximately 28 kilometres and look for signs to Sheaves Cove Beach and Hidden Falls. The road to the beach is a 0.5-kilometre-long gravel road that runs beside a private home on the left side of the highway.

AMENITIES: Outhouses, picnic tables, benches.

NEARBY: Ship Cove Beach (8 kilometres), Boutte du Cap Park (17 kilometres), Piccadilly Beach (19 kilometres).

WESTERN NEWFOUNDLAND

9 Piccadilly Beach

Piccadilly Beach is in Piccadilly Head Park, a former provincial park and campground that is now privately owned. To access the beach, take the path and staircase near the end of the gravel road that runs through the park. A day-use fee is required.

The beach stretches for approximately 1 kilometre from Piccadilly Park to just below the Parkview Variety convenience store on Route 463. As you travel from east to west, the character of the shoreline changes from sandy to very rocky. Interesting geological features are found at the western end of the beach, including the "Folded Rocks," layers of sandstone and shale that were curved and bent by tectonic forces hundreds of millions of years ago.

Be aware that features on the west side of the headland may be reachable only at low tide. Care should also be taken while navigating the rocks, as they can be quite slippery.

Photo © Linden Jesso

Photo © Linden Jesso

Piccadilly Beach is most impressive during low tide, when the ocean retreats to reveal expansive tidal flats. Tide times can be checked online at tideschart.com.

COORDINATES: 48.591515, -58.903680.

DIRECTIONS: From Stephenville, take Route 460 to the Port au Port Peninsula and turn onto Route 463 at Abrahams Cove. Continue on Route 463 for 7 kilometres to Piccadilly Park. Follow the gravel road through the park for 650 metres to the parking area above the beach.

AMENITIES: Unserviced campsites, rental cabins, outhouses, picnic tables, firepits.

NEARBY: Our Lady of Lourdes Grotto (13 kilometres), Sheaves Cove Beach and Hidden Falls (19 kilometres).

35

10 Cedar Cove

At Little Port in Lark Harbour, a 1.8-kilometre trail through boreal forest takes you to a scenic beach in a sheltered cove. Officially named "Wild (Capelin) Cove," it is known locally as Cedar Cove, and the trail is called the Cedar Cove Trail.

The hike to the beach is rated as easy to moderate because of its short distance with only slight changes in elevation, although many roots and rocks make the ground uneven in places. Conditions can also be muddy after wet weather.

Look for the trailhead at the back right corner of the parking area, where a steep staircase leads up the hill to the trail. At the first fork, follow the sign left toward Cedar Cove and stay on the main trail, as a side trail leads up the hill for a more challenging hike to Little Port Head.

Near the end of the trail, you will emerge from the brush onto a barren terrace surrounded by mountains. Note your location for the return hike, as it can be hard to spot; a rough sculpture constructed from wood and marine debris serves as a marker. Use caution when making your way down to the beach. The bank is steep with loose rocks and dirt.

Cedar Cove is a beachcomber's dream; heaps of driftwood accumulate below the banks, along with bits of old nets, rope, and other items washed ashore by the waves. With a view of the Gulf of St. Lawrence and many large boulders to sit on, the beach is an excellent spot to have a bonfire or picnic before heading back to Little Port.

COORDINATES: 49.106053, -58.421086 (trailhead and parking area); 49.090622, -58.423678 (beach).

DIRECTIONS: From the TCH, take Route 450 to Lark Harbour. Turn left at the convenience store and follow this road to Little Port. Park in the gravel lot across the road from the wharf. Take care not to block other vehicles or interfere with port operations.

AMENITIES: None.

NEARBY: Little Port Head Lighthouse Trail (<1 kilometre), Bottle Cove Beach (2 kilometres), Southhead Lighthouse Trail (2 kilometres), Blow Me Down Provincial Park (6 kilometres).

37

11 Bottle Cove

Accessible only by boat until 1961, Bottle Cove is now easily reachable by car for visitors interested in beach activities, picnicking, or hiking. Parking, picnic tables, and benches are located next to the beach.

Take a stroll along the 0.5-kilometre-long boardwalk that skirts the beach and visit a replica of the *Grenville*, the ship that Captain James Cook used to survey Newfoundland. At the end of the boardwalk, a 300-metre trail through the trees leads to the Trails End Monument, which marks the endpoint of Cook's mapping of the Bay of Islands.

Walk out onto the flat promontory—be mindful of the steep cliffs—for a view overlooking Bottle Cove on one side and the Gulf of St. Lawrence on the other. The spot offers a direct view of the sea cave on the south side of the cove, and it is touted as one of the best sites in Western Newfoundland to watch the sunset.

For those interested in exploring further, the path to Trails End joins up with a network of other hiking trails, including the 3.3-kilometre (one way) South Head Lighthouse Trail, which has an elevation gain of 350 metres and offers a breathtaking view of the Bay of Islands.

COORDINATES: 49.112960, -58.407619.

DIRECTIONS: From the TCH, take Route 450 to Lark Harbour and turn left onto Little Port Road, just past the convenience store. After approximately 2 kilometres, turn right onto Beacon Road and park next to the beach. A second parking area is 400 metres up the road.

AMENITIES: Picnic tables and benches.

NEARBY: South Head Lighthouse Trail (<1 kilometre), Cedar Cove Trail (2 kilometres), Little Port Head Lighthouse Trail (2 kilometres), Murray Mountain Trail (3 kilometres), Blow Me Down Provincial Park (5 kilometres).

WESTERN NEWFOUNDLAND

12 Blow Me Down Park

Crystal clear, shallow water makes the beach at Blow Me Down Provincial Park the perfect place to hunt for sand dollars, crabs, and starfish. The park is on a small peninsula separating Lark Harbour and York Harbour, with the beach at the southeast end of the park.

Jump in for a swim if you can tolerate the cold water, do some paddleboarding or boating, or just sit back and soak in the view of the Blow Me Down Mountains. At the north end of the beach, don't miss one of the main attractions: the Governor's Staircase. Built into the side of a cliff, the staircase ascends steeply from the beach under a ceiling of volcanic rock formed hundreds of millions of years ago.

At the top of the staircase, continue for a few hundred metres to a lookout offering a 360-degree view of the Bay of Islands. The path is part of the 4.5-kilometre James Cook Heritage Trail, which continues out to the top of Tortoise Mountain near the tip of the peninsula.

COORDINATES: 49.091761, -58.376425 (park entrance); 49.089775, -58.362695 (beach).

DIRECTIONS: From the TCH, take Route 450 for approximately 55 kilometres to Blow Me Down Provincial Park. The park is on the right just as you enter Lark Harbour, about 1.5 kilometres past the town sign. Follow the gravel road through the park for 1 kilometre to the large parking area next to the beach.

AMENITIES: Benches, picnic tables, and outhouses near the beach; a wheelchair-accessible bathroom in the campground.

NEARBY: Bottle Cove Beach (5 kilometres), Little Port Head Lighthouse Trail (6 kilometres), Cedar Cove Trail (6 kilometres), Copper Mine Falls Trail (11 kilometres).

Different theories exist about the origin of the name Blow Me Down. Local legend holds that in 1771, a sea captain named Messervey was anchoring his boat near the mountains in high winds when he exclaimed, "I hope they don't blow me down!" *Place Names of Atlantic Canada* claims that the name is a variation on "Blomidon," meaning a place where land rises steeply from the water. The mountains are known for their fierce winds, and they also rise abruptly from sea level to 750 metres, making both accounts plausible.

13 Pasadena Beach

Pasadena Beach is at the southern end of Deer Lake, in the town of Pasadena. In warm weather, the large freshwater lake with its sand and pebble shoreline draws swimmers, sunbathers, picnickers, boaters, and paddleboarders from Pasadena and surrounding areas.

Shade is scarce on the beach, so you may want to pack an umbrella or sunshade. Sandals are also useful as the sand–pebble mix can be rough on the feet, although the ground is softer underfoot in the water.

A popular feature on site is the Oasis Grillhouse, which serves food and drinks throughout the summer on a large deck overlooking the beach. It also offers takeout, but it may be closed on rainy days. Public volleyball courts are available at the east end of the beach near the restaurant (bring your own ball).

For a more serene experience, head to the quieter west end of the beach.

Salmon are sometimes spotted jumping in South Brook, a scheduled salmon river that empties into Deer Lake at this location.

COORDINATES: 49.022234, -57.608328.
DIRECTIONS: From Main Street in Pasadena, take 1st Avenue and then turn right onto Ryans Road (sign for Oasis Grillhouse). Drive approximately 0.5 kilometres and park in the large gravel lot in front of the beach.
AMENITIES: Picnic tables, restaurant.
NEARBY: Pasadena Ski and Nature Park (3 kilometres), Wright's Family Farm and Market (3 kilometres).

WESTERN NEWFOUNDLAND

14 Deer Lake Beach

From the Town of Deer Lake, the TCH runs southwest for more than 25 kilometres along the freshwater lake after which the town was named. The lake itself was named by early settlers for the caribou—mistaken as deer—that they encountered there.

Located in the heart of the town, Deer Lake Beach boasts 2 kilometres of golden-brown sand and shallow water, making it a favourite destination for local families with children. The lake is also popular with kayakers and paddleboarders, and those with motorized watercraft make use of the lake farther from the shore.

In front of the beach, adjacent to a large parking lot, a grassy area is dotted with picnic tables and benches. Wheelchair-accessible bathrooms are on the left as you enter the parking lot, and a ramp provides a path for wheelchairs down to the beach.

Walk along the partially wooded trail at the top of the beach to enjoy the shade while viewing the lake through the trees. Visible on the southeast shore is the century-old Deer Lake Powerhouse, which supplies hydroelectric power to the Corner Brook Pulp and Paper Mill. At the opposite end of the beach, an RV park (accessed via Park Lane) rents serviced and unserviced sites throughout the summer.

Past the RV park, the beach ends at the mouth of the Upper Humber River. An island at the site is an important habitat for waterfowl, including American black ducks, American wigeons, and ring-necked ducks, and there is also a stewardship area about 3.5 kilometres upriver.

COORDINATES: 49.178669, -57.442444.

DIRECTIONS: From the TCH, take Exit 15 into Deer Lake and get onto Nicholsville Road. The parking area for the beach is approximately 0.5 kilometres down Nicholsville Road on the left.

AMENITIES: Wheelchair-accessible bathrooms, picnic tables, benches, snack stand.

NEARBY: Roy Whalen Heritage Museum (2 kilometres), Humber River Trail (4 kilometres), Newfoundland Insectarium (4 kilometres), Humber River Golf Club (6 kilometres).

WESTERN NEWFOUNDLAND

15 Trout River Beach

The town of Trout River, with its grey sand-and-pebble beach, is nestled in a sheltered bay in the southern portion of Gros Morne National Park. The beach is a popular place for walks, especially on the raised boardwalk that runs beside colourful houses and fishing sheds. Weathered clapboard, boats, and stacked crab and lobster pots offer plenty of photograph opportunities.

Along the boardwalk is a small park with benches, picnic tables, and a sign recounting the story of "Big Blue," the Blue Whale that washed ashore on Trout River Beach in 2014. The reconstructed skeleton of Big Blue has been on display at the Royal Ontario Museum in Toronto since 2017.

At the northeast end of Main Street, climb the steep staircase to the top of the cliff overlooking the beach. From there, the trail continues for approximately 1 kilometre to Eastern Point. Hikers rave about the views of the craggy, rocky coastline—the same section of coast visible from the more strenuous Green Gardens Trail east of Trout River. At the southwest end of the town are two additional hiking trails as well as a boat launch, playground, picnic area, campground, and small pebble beach on a freshwater pond.

COORDINATES: 49.482174, -58.124703.

DIRECTIONS: From the TCH, take Route 430 to Wiltondale, turn left onto Route 431, and drive for 50 kilometres to Trout River. Watch the signs, as a sharp left is required just before Woody Point to stay on Route 431. Parking is available at the intersection of Main Street and Mountain Drive.

AMENITIES: Benches, picnic tables, tent platform on the Eastern Point Trail.

NEARBY: Lighthouse/Old Man Trail (<1 kilometre), Trout River Pond Trail (3 kilometres), Green Gardens Trail (4 kilometres), Tablelands Trail (12 kilometres).

WESTERN NEWFOUNDLAND

16 Old Man's Cove

Old Man's Cove, on the Green Gardens hiking trail, is on a stretch of coastline noteworthy for its soaring cliffs, lush meadows, and volcanic rock formations. The hike from Green Gardens trailhead on Route 431 to the beach is about 3.5 kilometres and is rated as moderately difficult due to an elevation change of approximately 400 metres. Most of the climbing occurs on the return trip.

At the cove, a steep wooden staircase takes you down over the cliffs to the beach for a closer look at the rock formations. If the tide is not too high, you can walk to the south end of the beach, where a tall waterfall empties into the ocean.

Beyond Old Man's Cove, the trail continues across the top of the cliffs for another kilometre to Steve's Cove. You may encounter sheep along the path, as the meadows are used as grazing pastures by residents of nearby Trout River. The Green

Photo © Julie Sircom

Gardens trail once continued beyond Steve's Cove to Wallace Brook and looped back to the highway from there, but that section was permanently closed in 2017 due to dangers caused by erosion.

COORDINATES: 49.4905, -58.07712 (trailhead and parking lot); 49.507241, -58.100785 (beach).

DIRECTIONS: From the TCH, take Route 430 and turn left onto Route 431 at Wiltondale. Just before Woody Point, make a sharp left to stay on Route 431 and drive for about 13 kilometres to the trailhead. Look for the sign "Green Gardens-Long Pond."

AMENITIES: Outhouses at trailhead and above beach; Adirondack chairs, tent platforms, and picnic tables on trail.

NEARBY*: Trout River Beach and Eastern Point Trail (4 kilometres), Trout River Pond Trail (6 kilometres), Tablelands Trail (8 kilometres), Lookout Trail (12 kilometres).

*Approximate distance from the trailhead.

WESTERN NEWFOUNDLAND

17 Western Brook Beach

One of the most popular destinations in Gros Morne National Park is the landlocked fjord at Western Brook Pond. Fewer people are aware of the white sandy beach just 5 kilometres north, where Western Brook empties into the Gulf of St. Lawrence.

As you enter the parking lot at Western Brook, look for the sign indicating the path to the beach on the left. The trail, which includes two steep wooden staircases, meanders along the brook and through the forest for approximately 200 metres before arriving at the long, curved sandbar and grass-covered dunes.

Due to erosion of the dunes, visitors are asked to remain on designated paths, and pets must be kept on leash. On the beach, walk near the shoreline rather than near the base of the dunes, as the site is also an important habitat for the endangered piping plover. Signs along the trail describe the loss of the species at Gros Morne, along with its continued recovery

in response to conservation efforts.

Swimming is not permitted at the beach due to a dangerous undertow, and camping is also not allowed. A picnic area, including a covered shelter, is in the grassy meadow adjacent to the parking lot.

COORDINATES: 49.828299, -57.855928 (trailhead and parking lot); 49.827263, -57.859391 (beach).

DIRECTIONS: From the TCH, take Route 430 for approximately 98 kilometres. The large, paved parking lot is just off the highway at Western Brook, 5 kilometres past the sign for the Western Brook Pond hiking trail and boat tours.

AMENITIES: Picnic area, outhouse.

NEARBY: Steve's Trail (2 kilometres), Broom Point Historical Exhibit (2 kilometres), Western Brook Pond hiking trail and boat tours (5 kilometres), wreck of the *Ethie* at Martin's Point (8 kilometres).

WESTERN NEWFOUNDLAND

18 Shallow Bay

Shallow Bay, in the northwest corner of Gros Morne National Park, attracts visitors with its long stretch of soft, pale sand, excellent amenities, and water that is shallow enough to reach comfortable temperatures in hot weather. Relatively narrow at high tide, the beach becomes significantly wider at low tide, leaving plenty of room to fly a kite, build sandcastles, or search for shells, sand dollars, and other treasures.

From the parking lot, it's a 200-metre walk to the beach on a flat, gravel pathway. At the end of the path, a wheelchair-accessible observation platform makes a good vantage point for watching the sunset, although you may want to bring along mosquito repellent.

Numerous seabirds and shorebirds inhabit the area, especially during the fall migration. Commonly spotted are sandpipers, plovers, sanderlings, gulls, terns, and cormorants, among many other avian species. Be careful not to disturb nests when walking near the dunes.

For visitors interested in a short, easy hike, the Old Mail Trail begins in the day-use area and continues for 1.2 kilometres through the woods behind the beach. A sign tells the history of the trail, which served as a route for postal delivery along the coast from 1882 to 1952. Use the boardwalk at the end of the trail to cross the dunes and make the return trip along the beach.

COORDINATES: 49.934748, -57.775191.

DIRECTIONS: From the TCH, take Route 430 to Cow Head and turn right on Parks Road; watch for signs for Shallow Bay. Where the pavement ends, stay left at the fork and drive approximately 350 metres to the large parking lot adjacent to the day-use area.

AMENITIES: Picnic tables, sheltered cookhouse, change rooms, bathrooms. A campground on site has additional amenities.

NEARBY: Old Mail Road Trail (<1 kilometre), Dr. Henry N. Payne Community Museum (4 kilometres), Cow Head Lighthouse (6 kilometres), Arches Provincial Park (20 kilometres).

WESTERN NEWFOUNDLAND

19 Arches Provincial Park

Most visitors to Arches Provincial Park, just north of Gros Morne, come to see the three connected rock archways shaped by glacial action and erosion. Many also find themselves charmed by the beach surrounding the arches, with its rounded cobbles in an endless variety of sizes, patterns, and colours.

The stones' shape can make them tricky to walk on because they roll around underfoot. Be especially careful when exploring below the arches during low tide, as the wet, algae-covered rocks are extremely slippery. For those with mobility challenges, a wheelchair-accessible picnic area overlooks the beach and provides a clear view of the beach and rock formation.

Adjacent to the picnic area is a large, paved lot with ample parking. Birdwatchers will appreciate the opportunity to spot woodpeckers, warblers, grouse, and other species in the dense tuckamore encircling the site. Another interesting feature is the

large stand of dead trees, twisted and bleached by the elements, located in the middle of the parking area.

Remember that provincial and national parks are protected areas. Refrain from climbing on the arches or removing stones and other materials from the beach. Another beach with similar stones is located at River of Ponds, 54 kilometres north. Arches Provincial Park is for day-use only; camping is not permitted,.

COORDINATES: 50.114346, -57.664558.

DIRECTIONS: From the TCH, take Route 430. The park is about 24 kilometres north of Cow Head, between Parson's Pond and Portland Creek. Watch for the sign, as the turnoff is easy to miss.

AMENITIES: Wheelchair-accessible outhouses and picnic area.

NEARBY: Portland Creek Beach (8 kilometres), Moulting Pond swimming area (11 kilometres), Mountain Waters Resort (13 kilometres), Shallow Bay Beach (20 kilometres).

WESTERN NEWFOUNDLAND

20 Portland Creek

The tiny town of Portland Creek, 25 kilometres north of Gros Morne National Park, has one of the rare sandy beaches on the Northern Peninsula. Compared with the other sandy beaches at Shallow Bay and Western Brook, this beach seems wilder, with larger accumulations of driftwood and seaweed. At low tide, boulders scattered throughout the cove become exposed as the water retreats, and flocks of gulls gather to feed along the shoreline.

Starting in front of the Entente Cordiale Inn at the north end of town, visitors can stroll along the sand for more than 1 kilometre before encountering the creek for which the town is named. Rubber boots are needed to cross the creek without getting wet, but those who do cross are rewarded with a closer view of the rolling dunes.

At the top of the creek is Portland Creek Pond, a narrow lake that extends inland for almost 20 kilometres. Kayakers and canoers interested in a long, challenging paddle can access the lake from the Mountain Waters Resort, 6 kilometres north of Portland Creek. Bring your own boat.

COORDINATES: 50.169744, -57.608717.

DIRECTIONS: From the TCH, take Route 430 to Portland Creek, approximately 143 kilometres. Head toward the water and then follow the road adjacent to the coastline for 1 kilometre to a small, gravel parking area. A short footpath leads to the beach.

AMENITIES: None.

NEARBY: Bill's Woods Trail (10 kilometres), Nurse Myra Bennett Heritage House (11 kilometres), Moulting Pond swimming area (19 kilometres).

WESTERN NEWFOUNDLAND

21 Port au Choix

Port au Choix is best known for its national historic site, where artifacts from ancient cultures, fossils of prehistoric animals, and rare plants can be viewed. Visitors to the site may also be interested in checking out one of the area's rocky beaches.

The highway into the town of Port au Choix runs beside a beachy coastline for more than 5 kilometres. There are several places to pull in, including a spot about 1 kilometre outside town next to a rough wooden fence decorated with colourful floats. Beachcombing enthusiasts will appreciate the driftwood and marine debris that wash ashore in this area.

Just as you enter Port au Choix is another beach at Oceanside RV Park. Adjacent to the camping area, the beach has a wide, west-facing view of the Gulf of St. Lawrence, making it an excellent location for watching the sun set. In the daylight, explore the beach's rock formations, boulders, and tidal pools.

In the centre of town is a third beach on Point Riche Road, where a swinging bench provides a fun place to sit and enjoy the view of Gargamelle Cove. North of the beach, continue up the hill for a view overlooking the cove. This road will also take you out to the national historic site and the Point Riche Lighthouse.

COORDINATES: 50.703392, -57.355713 (Gargamelle Cove); 50.696495, -57.349168 (Oceanside RV Park).

DIRECTIONS: From the TCH near Deer Lake, follow Route 430 N for 217 kilometres and then turn left onto Route 430-28. Continue another 14 kilometres to Port au Choix.

AMENITIES: Bench at Gargamelle Cove; amenities at Oceanside RV Park, including serviced and unserviced sites, picnic tables, firepits, dumping station, and wheelchair-accessible washrooms.

NEARBY*: Ben's Folk Art Studio (<1 kilometre), Barbace Cove Trail (2 kilometres), Port au Choix National Historic Site (2 kilometres), Point Riche Lighthouse (4 kilometres), Crow Head Walking Trail in Port Saunders (9 kilometres).

*Approximate distance calculated from Gargamelle Cove.

WESTERN NEWFOUNDLAND

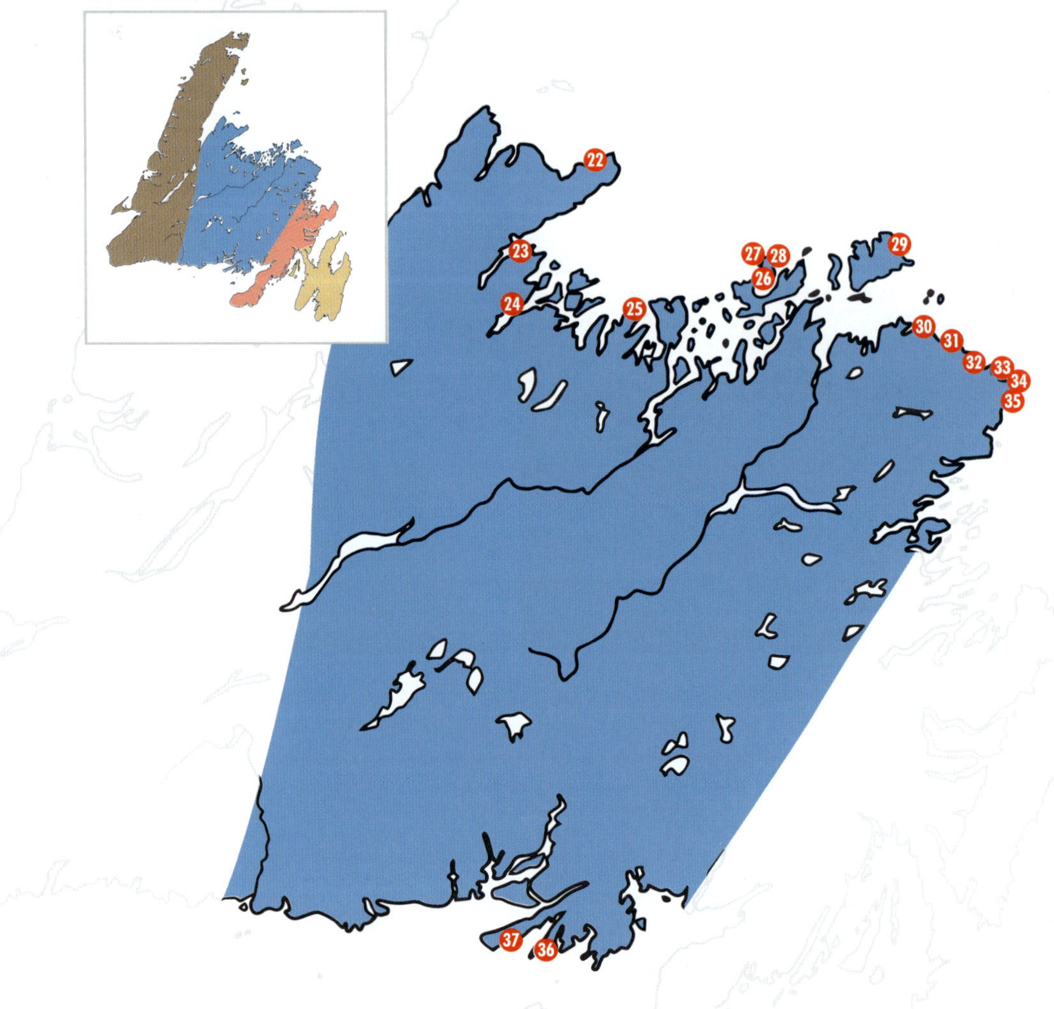

22	Island Cove		30	Musgrave Harbour
23	Nicky's Nose Cove		31	Banting Memorial Park
24	Glassy Beach		32	Deadman's Bay
25	Leading Tickles		33	Lumsden North
26	Back Harbour		34	Windmill Bight
27	Sleepy Cove		35	Cape Freels
28	French Beach & Spillers Cove		36	Deadman's Cove
29	Sandy Cove (Tilting)		37	Seal Cove Beach

Central Newfoundland

Central Newfoundland stretches eastward from the Baie Verte Peninsula to Cape Freels on the north coast of the island, and from just east of Burgeo to the Connaigre Peninsula on the south coast. The coastal geography varies widely within this area.

On the north shore, Notre Dame Bay is marked by deep inlets and small islands. Rugged and rocky, this region is not particularly known for its beaches. They do exist, however—mostly in the form of small, pocket beaches carved out of high cliffs or as narrow stretches of pebbles and cobbles with small amounts of coarse dark sand. While an occasional brave soul jumps in the water for a swim, the North Atlantic is usually prohibitively cold, and these beaches are more often appreciated as places to enjoy the scenery and fresh air, beachcomb for treasures, or gather with friends and family for a picnic or campfire.

East of Notre Dame Bay, the coastline changes. Almost no bays or harbours exist in the 45-kilometre stretch along Route 330 from Musgrave Harbour to Cape Freels, earning it the name the Straight Shore. This is one of the sandiest regions of Newfoundland, with long expanses of fine light sand backed by grass-covered dunes. Scientists believe that the large sand deposits are related to the shallow continental shelf in the area. Thousands of years ago, when sea levels were lower, sand would have accumulated on the exposed shelf as glacial sediment eroded. As sea levels rose, those beaches were destroyed and the sand carried onto the Straight Shore.

Some of the beaches along the Straight Shore, including the ones at Lumsden, are well known and attract visitors each summer seeking fun in the sand and surf. Others, such as those at Cape Freels, are less populated and act as important habitats for threatened or endangered bird species.

Situated as they are in Iceberg Alley, beaches along the north coast are excellent places to view icebergs in the spring and early summer as they are carried south from Greenland by the Labrador Current. Hiking opportunities also abound,

especially in the Twillingate area, where a large, interconnected network of trails passes alongside a variety of scenic rocky beaches. The strong tourism industry in this area, including that at Fogo Island, ensures the availability of a wide selection of accommodations, tours, shopping, and eating establishments.

The south coast is more remote and less developed in terms of tourism infrastructure. The drive from the TCH turnoff onto Route 360 to the tip of the Connaigre Peninsula is over 200 kilometres, most of it through a deserted wilderness with no gas stations and unreliable cell phone service. Be sure to fill your tank before heading out.

The Connaigre Peninsula is split by bays into three major sections accessed via different highways. Most amenities are found in the middle section at the end of Route 360 in Harbour Breton, which also boasts several sand and pebble beaches at Deadman's Cove. Down Route 364 on the western side of the peninsula, Seal Cove features a long barachois beach with soft, light sand. In addition to the beaches featured in this guide, on the eastern

side of the peninsula are many sand and pebble beaches near the communities dotting the coastline along Route 363. Some are next to the road; others are accessed via walking trails, such as the Stones Head Trail near Boxey and the Blue Pinion Trail near English Harbour West.

West of the Connaigre Peninsula, the coastline is inaccessible by car until you reach Burgeo, 130 kilometres away as the crow flies. Many of the communities that once existed here were abandoned years ago. Those that are still populated— Gaultois, McCallum, Francois, and Grey River—lie nestled among rocky cliffs and fjords, accessible by a coastal ferry service (passengers only) from Hermitage to Burgeo. Accommodations and other amenities in these communities are limited; make arrangements in advance.

22 Island Cove

The tip of the Baie Verte Peninsula, with its steep and rugged cliffs, does not seem a likely place to find a beach—but this is what makes Island Cove in La Scie so appealing. Tucked into a tiny cove carved out of the rock, the craggy beach is an excellent place to have a campfire, watch the sunset, or view boats as they come and go from La Scie Harbour.

Located on the northeast end of La Scie, the beach is inside Island Cove RV Park, which charges a small day-use fee. To access the beach, park at the far end of the campground, where a short path leads down to Island Cove. Near the parking area are trailheads for two hikes: Caplin Cove Trail runs across the top of the cliffs near the mouth of the harbour, and Lookout Trail goes up the hill east of the beach, which is an excellent vantage point for viewing icebergs and whales in season. If the climb seems too daunting, you can also drive to the lookout via a

gravel road just outside the park entrance.

In the town of La Scie is another small rocky beach, Morgan's Bawn, where French fishers salted and dried cod hundreds of years ago. To learn more about the history of the area—and perhaps grab a traditional Newfoundland meal—visit the Outport Museum and Tea Room.

COORDINATES: 49.967502, -55.606802.
DIRECTIONS: From the TCH, take Route 410 and then 414. In La Scie, turn right on Water Street and follow it to Island Cove RV Park. Park in the unpaved area past the campground and take the path down to the beach, about 100 metres.
AMENITIES: Canteen and store, serviced campsites and tenting areas, dumping station, showers, bathrooms.
NEARBY: Outport Museum and Tea Room (1 kilometre), remnants of copper mine at Tilt Cove (13 kilometres), walking trail and lookout at Harbour Round (16 kilometres).

CENTRAL NEWFOUNDLAND

23 Nicky's Nose Cove

Nicky's Nose Cove is a small cove backed by a beach in Green Bay, 23 kilometres from King's Point. On clear days, it offers a view across the bay to the Baie Verte Peninsula; on clear nights, the display of stars above the cove is impressive due to low levels of ambient light in the area.

The unpaved parking area at the east end of the beach is large enough to accommodate trailers and RVs. The trek to the other end of the beach is about 500 metres over coarse sand mixed with tiny pebbles. During caplin season, look closely at the sand to see thousands of round translucent eggs deposited by the fish, giving the ground along the shoreline a spongy quality. The fish typically wash ashore in the early morning or late evening.

If you prefer to walk on terra firma, the road runs alongside the top of the beach and has an unimpeded view of the cove. Picnic tables and benches on both ends of the beach provide spots to relax and have a snack while watching for whales.

COORDINATES: 49.693132, -55.969616.
DIRECTIONS: From the TCH, take Route 390 and then Route 391. Before reaching the town of King's Point, turn right toward Harry's Harbour and follow this road all the way to Nicky's Nose Cove.
AMENITIES: Picnic tables, benches.
NEARBY: Hiking trails and rocky beaches at Jackson's Cove (2 kilometres) and Harry's Harbour (4 kilometres).

CENTRAL NEWFOUNDLAND

24 Glassy Beach

At first glance, Glassy Beach near Springdale appears to be just another small, pebble beach carved into the coastline. Bordered by evergreens and clusters of reddish-brown conglomerate rock, it is pretty if not especially remarkable. A closer look, however, reveals thousands of sparkling, colourful fragments of sea glass among the pebbles.

The glass is the result of wave action that smoothed broken containers deposited there when the area served as a garbage dumping site. As of 2023, the sea glass was mostly white or green, with rare pieces of blue, yellow, and other colours. Long-time residents can remember when the glass was much more plentiful, before people began collecting it in large amounts. A sign at the beginning of the trail to the beach asks visitors to refrain from taking the glass, so that others can also enjoy it.

The trail to the beach is short (about 125 metres) but rough in places, with exposed roots, stumps, and rocks. The final descent requires climbing over large boulders. Take the side trail that veers off to the right near the end of the main trail for a gentler descent to the beach.

COORDINATES: 49.515769, -56.013532 (parking area and trailhead); 49.514792, -56.013904 (beach).

DIRECTIONS: From the TCH, take Route 390 toward Springdale and drive 15 kilometres to the end of the pavement. Follow the unpaved road for another 700 metres to a small parking area on the left. The trail to the beach is across the road from the parking area.

AMENITIES: Picnic table.

NEARBY: Indian River Walking Trail (6 kilometres), Indian River Falls (8 kilometres).

69

25 Leading Tickles

The beaches at Oceanview Park in Leading Tickles exemplify the coastal environment for which Newfoundland is best known: rugged cliffs, dark green hills, and waves churning around craggy rocks. The beaches are in two coves on either side of the park: East Bear Cove and West Bear Cove. At the park entrance, turn left at the kiosk and drive for about 20 metres to reach the turnoffs for the two beaches. There is a small fee to enter the park.

Both beaches have benches, picnic tables, and gazebos. At East Bear Cove, walk to the far end of the beach and scramble up and over the rocks to reach another, sandier beach with a small sea stack. At West Bear Cove, a 1-kilometre out-and-back trail leads to a lookout which offers a panoramic view of the area.

A full-service campground, Oceanview Park offers sites for RVs and tents, many on a grassy area next to the beach. Fanciful wood carvings of human and animal figures are a fun addition to the

park, and children will also enjoy the large playground. Two additional rocky beaches are found along the Oceanside Nature Trail, a hiking area at the western end of Leading Tickles.

COORDINATES: 49.510879, -55.445937 (East Bear Cove); 49.510224, -55.449968 (West Bear Cove).

DIRECTIONS: From the TCH, take Route 350 and drive approximately 70 kilometres to Park Road in Leading Tickles. Oceanview Park is about 500 metres down Park Road.

AMENITIES: Benches, picnic tables, bathrooms, store, and laundry.

NEARBY: Oceanside Nature Park and Hiking trail (2 kilometres), Giant Squid Interpretation site at Glover's Harbour (10 kilometres).

71

26 Back Harbour

On the west side of North Twillingate Island, Back Harbour is a popular spot to watch the sun set over Notre Dame Bay. At the base of the harbour, a narrow, pebble beach runs alongside Wild Cove Road. The beach looks out onto a small island just outside the harbour called Back Harbour Gull Island (to distinguish it from Sleepy Cove Gull Island farther north).

At the south end of the beach, where Wild Cove Road turns right onto Dock Road, take the path up the hill to sit on a bench and view the harbour. A short walk down Dock Road takes you to fishing stages and an abandoned dory, a reminder of the area's past.

Just beyond the stages, a 1.3-kilometre trail leads out to Batrix Island (also known as Barrick's Island) via a tombolo beach. There are also narrow beaches to explore on the flat portion of the island before the path climbs to Batrix Head for a panoramic view.

From Back Harbour, it is a short drive to two more pebble beaches at Wild Cove and Little Wild Cove. Many secluded rocky beaches are also found along the area's ATV trails, such as at Dumpling Cove, just below the cemetery at the end of St. Peter's Church Road/Sellens Cove Road.

COORDINATES: 49.659921, -54.787738.

DIRECTIONS: Follow Route 340 through Twillingate to Back Harbour. Take Back Harbour Road to Wild Cove Road and park on the side of the road. Alternatively, park near the Batrix Island Trail, but be respectful of private property and fishing operations.

AMENITIES Benches; other amenities nearby at Peyton's Woods RV Park and Campground including bathrooms, showers, and canteen.

NEARBY: Twillingate Museum (1 kilometre), Smith's Lookout (2 kilometres), Sleepy Cove (5 kilometres), Long Point Lighthouse (5 kilometres).

Photo © Paula Burt

Photo © Paula Burt

Photo © Paula Burt

In 1966, two brothers in Back Harbour discovered stone artifacts while digging a hole for an outhouse. Further archaeologic excavations uncovered items associated with the Maritime Archaic tradition at several locations, including a cemetery. The site is referred to as the Curtis Site, after the brothers.

73

27 Sleepy Cove

Sleepy Cove, near Crow Head, was the site of a copper mine in the early 20th century. The mine closed in 1917, but visitors can view machinery remnants on a point of land above the cove. From there, a narrow footpath leads down the hill to the rocky beach.

Sheltered by the surrounding hills, the beach is an ideal spot for picnics and campfires. Rugged cliffs and offshore rocks provide a scenic backdrop for photographs. The best place to spot whales and icebergs is atop the cliffs, which offer an expansive view of Notre Dame Bay. Just outside the cove is Sleepy Cove Gull Island, home to thousands of gulls, black guillemots, terns, and puffins.

The beach lies roughly near the middle of a 6.4-kilometre hiking trail that runs along the northwest portion of North Twillingate Island and includes loops and side trails. From the beach, head north to reach the Long Point Lighthouse and a coastal feature

called Nanny's Hole. During tourist season, the lighthouse offers a *Titanic* exhibit (for a small admission fee), and visitors rave about the homemade fudge sold in the gift shop. Hiking southward from the beach, the trail leads to Lower Head, where a 3-kilometre loop around the headland offers shifting panoramic views.

COORDINATES: 49.682628, -54.803010 (turnoff to Sleepy Cove on Route 340); 49.684576, -54.806630 (beach).

DIRECTIONS: Follow Route 340 through Twillingate and north to Lighthouse Road on North Twillingate Island. About 500 metres before the lighthouse is an unpaved road on the left with a sign for the hiking trails. Sleepy Cove is about 200 metres down the dirt road.

AMENITIES: Picnic tables, serviced campground with rental bunkies (under development).

NEARBY: Wild Cove (3 kilometres), Batrix Island Trail in Back Harbour (5 kilometres), Twillingate Museum (5 kilometres).

CENTRAL NEWFOUNDLAND

28 French Beach & Spillers Cove

French Beach is in Durrell near the town of Twillingate, at the start of a 7-kilometre hiking loop between French Beach and Spillers Cove (not to be confused with Spillars Cove, Bonavista). The trail makes a gradual ascent through a barren, rocky landscape for about 300 metres. Near the top of the hill, French Beach, covered in pink granite cobbles and pebbles, comes into view. Watch your footing on the loose gravel as you head down the hill.

To continue to Spillers Cove, cross the beach and follow the trail around the headland. At Spillers Cove, a steep staircase leads down to a rocky beach surrounded by high cliffs and sea stacks ("spillers"). Look for ospreys, which are known to nest here. From Spillers Cove, the trail heads inland to complete the loop. Spillers Cove can also be accessed more directly from Dump Road in Durrell. About a kilometre down the road, follow the trail on the left just beyond the parking area. Watch for the sign, which is small and easy to miss.

The French Beach to Spillers Cove hike is part of the Rockcut Trail System, 25 kilometres of interconnected trails on the east side of South Twillingate Island. Rocky beaches are found at other points along these trails, including Codjack's Cove, Little Harbour, Jones Cove, and Purcells Cove. At the abandoned community of Little Harbour, trail highlights include a root cellar and a natural sea arch.

COORDINATES: 49.668583, -54.728134 (parking area and trailhead); 49.671521, -54.725587 (French Beach); 49.664114, -54.719010 (Spillers Cove).

DIRECTIONS: As you enter Twillingate on Route 340, turn right onto Main Street and drive to the end of the pavement in Durrell. Near Blow Me Down Lane is a small parking area and the trailhead for the French Beach to Spillers Cove hike.

AMENITIES: Camping platform on the trail.

NEARBY: Durrell Museum (3 kilometres), Isles Boat Museum (7 kilometres).

CENTRAL NEWFOUNDLAND

29 Sandy Cove (Tilting)

Visitors to Fogo Island may be surprised to discover a white sandy beach in the largely barren, rocky landscape on the north shore of the island. Just over 1 kilometre from the historic town of Tilting, Sandy Cove Beach is a favourite swimming spot for locals in fine weather. In not-so-fine weather, watch the waves roll ashore or crash against the rocks on either side of the cove. Shorebirds, including yellowlegs, are spotted throughout the summer. Look for icebergs in late spring, and whales from spring to fall.

An 8-kilometre hiking trail called Turpin's Trail wraps around Sandy Cove and beyond. On the eastern side of the cove, the trail extends almost 5 kilometres along the coastline to Tilting's oldest home, the Lane House Museum. On the western side, the trail begins west of the parking area at a small footbridge next to the highway. This portion of the trail makes a 3-kilometre loop out to Sandy Cove Point and past two smaller beaches before heading inland and back toward the highway. Turpin's Trail, as well as Turpin's

Rock at Sandy Cove Beach, are named after a resident of Tilting who reportedly lost his head (literally) in a skirmish with Beothuk near the site in 1809.

COORDINATES: 49.708453, -54.082288.
DIRECTIONS: On Fogo Island, follow Route 334 toward Tilting. The unpaved parking area for the beach is just off the highway on the left, about 1 kilometre before Tilting.
AMENITIES: Change rooms, bathrooms, picnic tables, benches.
NEARBY: Historic Tilting (1 kilometre), Oliver's Cove Walking Trail (2 kilometres).

Tilting is a designated national historic site and registered heritage district, in recognition of its many surviving historical elements that illustrate the traditional way of life in outport Newfoundland. These include houses, community and commercial buildings, fishing structures, fenced gardens, paths, and cemeteries. Many of its current residents descended from Irish families who settled in the area more than 300 years ago.

30 Musgrave Harbour

Musgrave Harbour has 7 kilometres of sandy beach stretching along the northeast coast. Its vastness is exaggerated further by the wide grass-covered banks and flats that extend up to 200 metres between the beach and the town. Sunsets are spectacular, as the low-lying landscape makes the sky appear immense.

A sculptural wooden lounger—a dedication to a local resident—offers a comfortable place to rest and reflect. Look for icebergs in the spring, or take a dip to cool off on hot summer days.

The beach, sometimes called Doting Cove Beach, begins behind the Fisherman's Museum at 239 Main Road. Built in 1910, the museum is open throughout the summer and houses exhibits on the Newfoundland fishing industry. Don't miss the large painted mural on the outside of the building depicting changing fishing traditions.

Approximately 2 kilometres down the beach is a swimming area on the river called Big Brook (also accessible via Seaview Drive). A bridge across the brook forms part of the Sir Frederick Banting Walking Trail, which begins at the Fisherman's Museum and traverses 5 kilometres of beach and marshland before ending in Banting Memorial Municipal Park.

COORDINATES: 49.449588, -53.942707.
DIRECTIONS: From the TCH, take either Route 320 near Gambo or Route 330 at Gander to Musgrave Harbour. Follow Main Road to its intersection with Marine Drive and park next to the Fisherman's Museum. The beach is directly behind the museum.
AMENITIES: None.
NEARBY: Marine Drive Hiking Trail (<1 kilometre, at the end of Marine Drive), Banting Memorial Municipal Park (6 kilometres).

CENTRAL NEWFOUNDLAND

Banting Memorial Park

31

Banting Memorial Municipal Park is a short drive from Musgrave Harbour along Route 330. Visitors come in the summer to enjoy the fine white sand, camp at the campground, or avail of the park's other services and attractions. Try your hand at miniature golf or rent a paddleboat and take a spin around the pond near the beach.

If you are up for a short hike, the Sir Frederick Banting Walking Trail follows the scenic coastline for 4 to 5 kilometres to the edge of Musgrave Harbour. The trail includes several rest stops and signs recounting the area's history. A wheelchair-accessible ramp leads from the parking area to a lookout with a view of the beach and ocean.

Sir Frederick Banting was one of several scientists who discovered insulin in the early 1920s. Banting died in a plane crash just outside Musgrave Harbour in 1941, and a monument and interpretation centre in the park tell his story. The monument includes a reproduction of the plane and wreckage salvaged from the crash site. A day-use fee for the park and a fee to visit the interpretation centre are required.

COORDINATES: 49.418790, -53.877636.

DIRECTIONS: From the TCH, take either Route 320 near Gambo or Route 330 at Gander. Banting Memorial Municipal Park is off Route 330, 4 kilometres southeast of Musgrave Harbour.

AMENITIES: Bathrooms, showers, laundry, canteen, picnic area, serviced and unserviced campsites.

NEARBY: Musgrave Harbour Beach (6 kilometres), Fisherman's Museum (6 kilometres), Deadman's Bay Provincial Park (19 kilometres).

CENTRAL NEWFOUNDLAND

32 Deadman's Bay

Deadman's Bay Beach is a pristine, 2.5-kilometre bar of fine white sand located in Deadman's Bay Provincial Park, between the communities of Lumsden and Deadman's Bay. The beach is the perfect place to picnic, take a leisurely stroll, or just relax on the sand and watch the clouds float by. In spring and early summer, look for icebergs drifting down Iceberg Alley.

On clear nights, enjoy a spectacular view of the stars, owing to the low level of artificial light in the area. Birdwatchers will enjoy the opportunity to spot a wide variety of species on the beach and throughout the park, including bald eagles, turnstones, and terns. Dogs are permitted on the beach but should be leashed.

The shortest and most direct path to the beach is via a small, unpaved parking lot off Main Street in the town of Deadman's Bay. The entrance to the provincial park is off Route 330 south of the town. However, the walk to the beach is longer from that location and access to the beach is more difficult due to a gap in the sandbar.

COORDINATES: 49.346279, -53.702003 (turnoff to parking area and trailhead); 49.344875, -53.700447 (beach).

DIRECTIONS: From the TCH, take Route 320 toward Gambo or Route 330 from Gander. Follow the highway until you see a sign indicating the town of Deadman's Bay. Turn onto Main Street and watch for a turnoff into a small, unpaved parking area on the right, approximately 670 metres from the highway. Walk the short path (100 metres) through the bushes to the beach.

AMENITIES: None.

NEARBY: Deadman's Bay Mountain Bike and ATV Trail (2 kilometres), Lumsden beaches (12 kilometres).

CENTRAL NEWFOUNDLAND

33 Lumsden North

The town of Lumsden features several white sandy beaches near one another, the most well known of which is Lumsden North Beach. At almost 200 metres from the banks to the shoreline, this beach is so large that rows of vehicles parked on the beach leave ample room for visitors to spread out and enjoy the sand and surf. Fly a kite, go for a run, play frisbee—there is plenty of space.

Amenities are plentiful and add to the comfort of a day at the beach. A building with change rooms, showers, and bathrooms is located on the grassy bank behind the beach, and food is available for purchase. Have a game of volleyball, visit the playground, or take pictures by the large, multicoloured Lumsden sign. An area with 30 unserviced lots permits overnight camping.

At the south end of the beach, the flat expanse of sand turns into clusters of rocks and large grass-covered mounds.

Follow the walking trail through this area to Lumsden South Beach. A third beach, Back Beach, lies west of Lumsden North Beach and is accessible via ATV and walking trails. The Lumsden beaches form portions of the 8.5-kilometre Shoreline Walking Trail that also connects with a popular beach at Windmill Bight Park.

COORDINATES: 49.308971, -53.611375 (Lumsden North Beach); 49.299886, -53.598834 (Lumsden South Beach); 49.314729, -53.617888 (Back Beach).

DIRECTIONS: In the town of Lumsden, take Memorial Drive and follow the signs for the beach to Northside Road. Follow the unpaved road 100 metres to the beach. Cross a small bridge to enter Lumsden Park and take the first road on the right to the parking area.

AMENITIES: Change rooms, showers, bathrooms, food stand, campground, picnic tables.

NEARBY: Windmill Bight Park (6 kilometres), Deadman's Bay Provincial Park (9 kilometres).

CENTRAL NEWFOUNDLAND

34 Windmill Bight

Windmill Bight Beach is a 500-metre-long barachois beach in Windmill Bight Park, south of Lumsden. Farther back from the water is a strip of large, rounded stones in varying pastel hues, giving the beach a unique aesthetic. The stones are difficult to walk on as they slide around underfoot, but you can walk the sandy shoreline to enjoy the scenery and fresh ocean air. At the western end of the beach, large clusters of reddish-brown rocks complement the blue of water and sky.

Although some people swim or surf here, a sign posted near the beach warns of a dangerous undertow. Use caution if you venture into the water, or swim in the pond next to the parking area instead. Change rooms, outhouses, and picnic tables are located next to the pond. The park has a playground, canteen, and campsites for tents and recreational vehicles; a small day-use fee is required.

COORDINATES: 49.278013, -53.561951.

DIRECTIONS: From the TCH, take Route 320 and drive north approximately 90 kilometres to Windmill Bight Park. Follow the gravel road to the end and park next to the pond. The beach is just over the hill along a sandy path.

AMENITIES: Change rooms, outhouses, picnic tables, serviced and unserviced campsites.

NEARBY: Beaches at Lumsden (6 kilometres) and Cape Freels (9 kilometres).

CENTRAL NEWFOUNDLAND

35 Cape Freels

The beaches at Cape Freels in New-Wes-Valley are striking with their fine white sand, grass-covered dunes, and large outcroppings of pink and grey granite. Less well known than the beaches at Lumsden and other communities to the northeast, they are also less populated. At times, you may be sharing the space with only the numerous birds that nest and feed in the area, including piping plovers, red knots, and short-eared owls. Cape Freels is one of the richest bird areas in Newfoundland, and efforts are being made to protect the beaches, dunes, and other habitats that support these and other species at risk.

The largest beach is Cape Island Beach, located in Cape Cove along the 6-kilometre southern loop of the Cape Island Hiking Trail. The trail begins in a parking lot off Beach Road and passes alongside a pond before veering left at a fork toward the beach. The beach is approximately

1 kilometre from the trailhead, and another 1.5 kilometres south along the beach brings you to Cape Island, beyond which lies another long stretch of sand.

The site of a community settled in the late 1700s and then abandoned in the mid–1900s, Cape Island was the setting for the novel *Random Passage* by Bernice Morgan. Artifacts from various early Indigenous groups, including Maritime Archaic Indians and Dorset Paleoeskimos, have been found at the beach.

In addition to Cape Island Beach, a smaller but more readily accessible sandy beach runs alongside Beach Road in Cape Freels South, near the United Church cemetery and old church foundation. Another sandy beach is adjacent to the wharf in town at Cape Freels North. Small rocky beaches lie along the northern loop of the hiking trail, on the headland north of Cape Island Beach.

COORDINATES: 49.243304, -53.483507 (Cape Island Beach); 49.254521, -53.494793 (beach by church foundation); 49.260137, -53.497159 (beach by wharf).

DIRECTIONS: From the TCH, take Route 320 toward Gambo/New-Wes-Valley and drive 90 kilometres to Cape Freels Road. Turn right, drive 4 kilometres, and then take the unpaved Beach Road. Just over 1 kilometre down Beach Road is the parking area and trailhead for Cape Island Trail. Walk the remaining 1 kilometre to the beach along the trail, turning left at the fork after the small bridge.

AMENITIES: None.

NEARBY: Queens Meade Wetlands (7 kilometres), Barbour Living Heritage Village (14 kilometres), Pool's Island Lookout (19 kilometres).

36 Deadman's Cove

Deadman's Cove in Harbour Breton includes four adjacent coves with sand and pebble beaches; from east to west: Chappie Cove, Black Island Cove, and two beaches at Western Cove separated by a rock outcropping.

At Chappie Cove, take the wooden staircase down to a covered lookout, which offers views of the beach and offshore islands. The two small islands closest to shore, Gull Island and Black Island, are nesting grounds for seabirds, including terns, gulls, and cormorants. On a clear day, you can see Sagona Island about 10 kilometres offshore, the larger Brunette Island beyond it, and sometimes even the French island of Miquelon over 50 kilometres away. Sagona and Brunette Islands, once home to hundreds of inhabitants, were abandoned in the 1960s.

From the lookout, follow the footpath to the bottom of the meadow and down

CENTRAL NEWFOUNDLAND

a stairway past chunks of the same red granite seen in Red Head, the 150-metre-high mass on the eastern side of the cove. Walk to the end of the beach and, if the water is not too high, cross the triangular sandbar to Black Island Cove.

To access Western Cove from Black Island Cove, climb the long, steep staircase near the western end of the beach. The staircase leads to Deadman's Cove Beach Trail, which begins at Chappie Cove and follows the coast for 2 kilometres before veering inland to loop around Mile Pond. The total length is 3.8 kilometres and includes several steep staircases. Western Cove can also be accessed by hiking in from the Mile Pond Boardwalk Trail, which begins near the entrance to Harbour Breton and includes a side trail toward the beach about halfway around the pond.

COORDINATES: 47.459544, -55.836657 (Chappie Cove); 47.462062, -55.839934 (Black Island Cove); 47.469032, -55.850986 (Western Cove); 47.477898, -55.847940 (Mile Pond Boardwalk trailhead).

DIRECTIONS: From the TCH, take Route 360 into Harbour Breton. Turn right on Deadman's Cove Road (sign for Deadman's Cove Park). Follow this unpaved road for approximately 1 kilometre to the parking area, past a swimming pond, campground, and two cemeteries.

AMENITIES: Picnic tables, gazebo/lookout, and an RV park with serviced sites, bathrooms, showers, and laundry.

NEARBY: Sunny Cottage Heritage Centre (3 kilometres), Connaigre Trail (3 kilometres), Rocky Point Lighthouse Trail (4 kilometres), Gunn Hill Lookout Trail (4 kilometres).

CENTRAL NEWFOUNDLAND

37 Seal Cove

The long, sandy beach at Seal Cove, Fortune Bay, is in a cove referred to as "The Bight," approximately 4 kilometres northeast of the town. Access to the beach is from Albert Loveless Memorial Day Park, dedicated to a late resident, teacher, and former mayor of Seal Cove. Parking is available in the unpaved lot at the park entrance; or drive approximately 300 metres down the gravel road to a second parking area next to a large barachois called Big Barasway. From there, an ATV and hiking trail leads 500 metres to the beach.

On the beach, watch for shorebirds, gather driftwood or seaweed, or just sink your feet into the soft sand and enjoy the view. Look for Connaigre Head across the bay, Brunette Island to the southeast, and the French island of Miquelon to the southwest. Crossing over the grassy banks at the east end of the beach brings you to a cobble beach and another, smaller, barachois beach at Little Barasway.

You may want to check out the smaller sandy beach near the wharves in Sandyville or the rocky beach at Partridge Cove in Hermitage-Sandyville Municipal Park. The park, which boasts a waterfall, has unserviced campsites, picnic tables, and outhouses.

COORDINATES: 47.503056, -56.027778 (Albert Loveless Park, parking and trailhead); 47.495973, -56.030658 (beach).

DIRECTIONS: From the TCH, take Route 360 and then Route 364 toward Hermitage-Sandyville. About 9 kilometres past Sandyville, look for the turnoff into the Albert Loveless Memorial Day Park on the left.

AMENITIES: Benches and picnic tables in the parking areas.

NEARBY: Sandyville Beach (9 kilometres), Hermitage Cove Lookout (12 kilometres), Hermitage-Sandyville Municipal Park (14 kilometres).

CENTRAL NEWFOUNDLAND

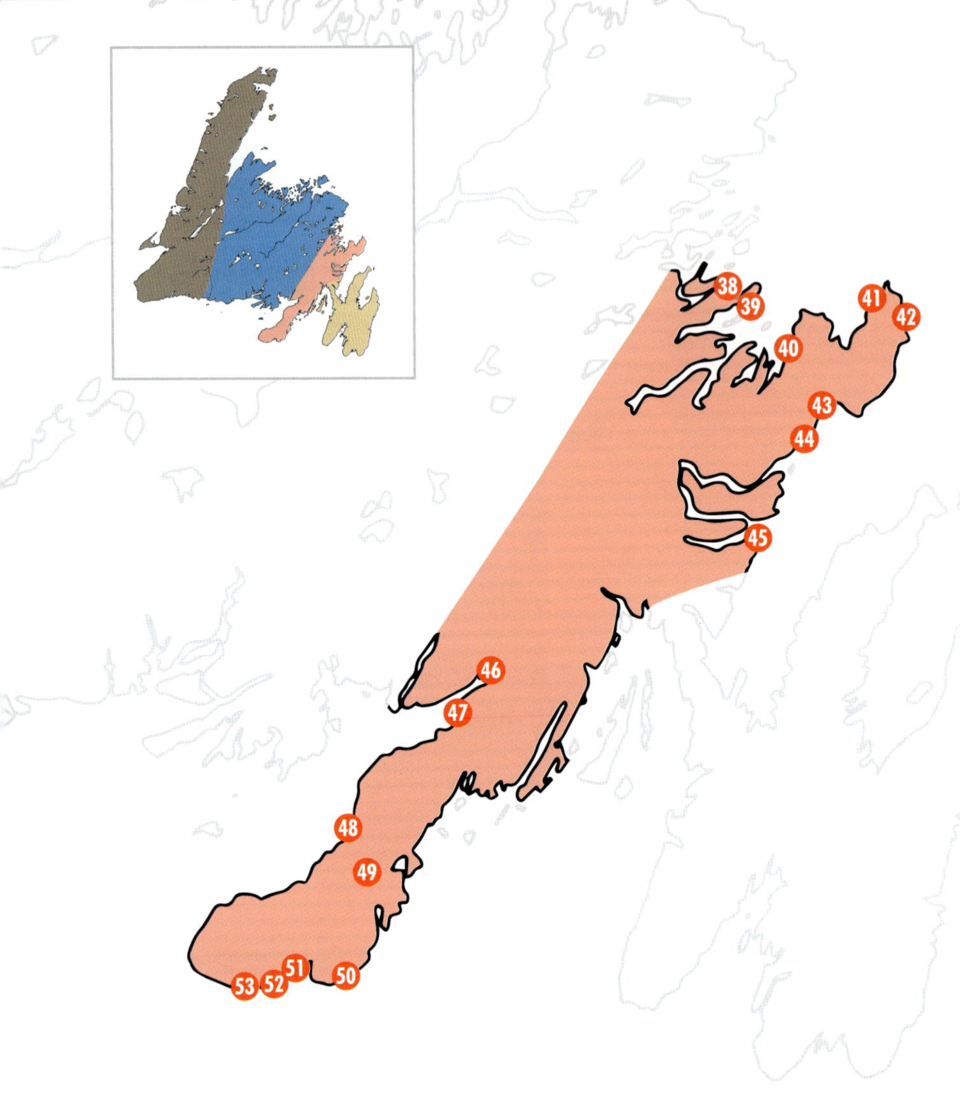

38	Eastport	46	Terrenceville Beach
39	Sandy Cove (Eastport)	47	Broad Cove Beach
40	Naked Man Beach	48	Frenchman's Cove
41	Long Beach	49	Golden Sands
42	Sandy Cove (Elliston)	50	Shoal Cove
43	Port Rexton Area	51	Backcove Beach
44	Sam White's Cove	52	Sandy Cove (Lord's Cove)
45	Heart's Ease Beach	53	Point au Gaul Strand

Eastern Newfoundland

Eastern Newfoundland encompasses the Eastport, Bonavista, and Burin peninsulas. Also included is the section of coastline just south of the Bonavista Peninsula, from Random Island to the southwest arm of Trinity Bay.

From the TCH, Route 310 (the Road to the Beaches) runs the length of the Eastport Peninsula. The main beaches are in the towns of Eastport and Sandy Cove, just 2 kilometres apart on opposite sides of the peninsula's narrowest point. With long, sandy shorelines, good swimming conditions, and easy access to amenities, these beaches are busy throughout the summer. Outside of this area, beaches are scarce, with the coastline consisting mainly of steep cliffs or heavily forested areas. Nevertheless, some smaller beaches exist, including a narrow sand and gravel beach in Happy Adventure and a small, pebble beach southwest of Salvage at Wild Cove. Terra Nova National Park, which extends into the lower portion of the peninsula, also has a small, shallow beach in a day-use area on Sandy Pond.

The Eastport Peninsula is the self-proclaimed Festival Capital of Newfoundland and Labrador. Visitors are drawn there not just by its beaches but also by its plentiful cultural events, art exhibits, musical performances, and family activities. The festival tradition is a legacy from 1969, when the provincial government encouraged the regional development of festivals to boost tourism. Many of the events are held at the Beaches Arts and Heritage Centre in Eastport or on one of the sandy beaches nearby.

The Bonavista Peninsula is accessed via Route 230 or Discovery Trail, in reference to John Cabot's first North American landfall there in 1497. Running mostly inland for the first third of the peninsula, the highway splits at Southern Bay to loop around the top of the peninsula, with several beaches along the route. The most accessible sandy beach is adjacent to the road in Elliston, and two more at the end of hiking trails in Plate Cove West. Other beaches on the peninsula sport various combinations of sand, pebbles, and cobbles, with many lying along spectacular coastal hiking trails.

The Bonavista Peninsula's booming tourism industry is based on its history and coastal scenery. The Cape Bonavista lighthouse, which operates as a museum, is one of the oldest in the province, and the town of Bonavista has well-preserved historic properties. Towering cliffs, sea stacks, and rugged shorelines leave visitors in awe, and you can get closer to puffins on land in Elliston than anywhere in North America.

Just below the Bonavista Peninsula, the highway has several side roads leading out toward the coast, with more small towns to explore and beaches to discover. Route 231 takes you to Random Island via a causeway built on a naturally occurring gravel bar. Beaches occur in or near almost every community on the island, with most containing some mixture of sand and rocks. One beach near Snook's Harbour has an unusual makeup: it is covered in fragments of red brick from a brick-making operation that closed in 1952. Below Random Island, Routes 204 and 205 follow the shorelines on opposite sides of Southwest Arm, an inlet of Trinity Bay. Noteworthy in this area is Heart's Ease Beach, a tombolo beach in Gooseberry Cove.

The Burin Peninsula, bounded on the west by Fortune Bay and on the east by Placentia Bay, is often described as the "The Boot" because of its shape. Marystown is about 140 kilometres from the TCH, down Route 210 (the Heritage Run). Side roads along the way lead to scenic outport communities, some of which have only been accessible by road for a few decades. Opportunities also exist to travel by passenger ferry to still-isolated outports, such as Rencontre East.

The beaches along this route are found mostly in communities clustered around a narrow inlet at the top of the peninsula in Fortune Bay. Although the Placentia Bay side of the peninsula is mostly rugged with high cliffs and few harbours, some beaches

occur north of Marystown, including a long sandy beach called Wild Beach, accessed via a gravel road just south of Jean de Baie.

South of Marystown, the highway loops around the bottom of the peninsula for 170 kilometres. Between St. Lawrence and Lamaline, several beaches draw visitors with their wide expanses of soft, light sand and some of the best surfing conditions on the island. As you move around the toe of the boot near Point May and then up into Fortune Bay, much of the coastline is lined with long, narrow stretches of sand and gravel punctuated with barachois beaches. One striking example is Grand Beach: a reddish beach which arcs around a large lagoon and beyond for more than 4.5 kilometres.

On a pleasant summer day, it is difficult to imagine how the bays, coves, and beaches encountered along this route could be anything but delightful. However, the Burin Peninsula has had its share of tragedies caused by harsh weather and angry seas. At Port au Bras near Burin, a memorial honours the victims of a devastating tsunami that struck the southeast portion of the peninsula in 1929. The result of an offshore earthquake and landslide, the tsunami took 27 lives and caused up to $1 million in property damage. Thirteen years later, two US naval ships, *Truxton* and *Pollux*, ran aground the same morning near St. Lawrence during a violent winter storm. More than 200 perished, but 183 were saved by the brave action of miners who worked at the local fluorspar mine. A memorial recounting the event is installed along a hiking trail at Chambers Cove.

38 Eastport

Eastport Beach is popular year-round for walking and admiring the scenery. In warmer weather, enjoy swimming, sunbathing, boating, and volleyball. Ample parking is available in a large, unpaved lot adjacent to the beach.

Two covered picnic shelters provide protection from the elements in poor weather. Another covered shelter is on a hill above the beach, offering a view of Eastport Bay. To reach this lookout, walk to the south end of the beach and scramble up and over the rocks. Alternatively, walk or drive south on the road for approximately 50 metres until you see a small gravel pull-in, where you will find a short path to the structure.

At the north end of Eastport Beach is the High Tide Trail, a 700-metre coastal path with boardwalk that leads to a more secluded beach at North Arm Provincial Park. This is Northside Beach, also known as Eastport Beach North. The trail can become impassable when the tide is high, and an alternative route between the beaches is along Bank Road, which runs parallel to the trail through the town of Eastport.

Both Eastport Beach and Northside Beach are wheelchair accessible, with accessibility ramps onto the beach and heavy, specialized mats, called MobiMats, laid out on the sand.

COORDINATES: 48.65105, -53.74875 (Eastport Beach); 48.659953, -53.758818 (Northside Beach).

DIRECTIONS: From the TCH, take Route 310 and drive almost 19 kilometres. The entrance to the parking area is a sharp left turn off Route 310. Northside Beach can be reached directly by car at Clay Cove, off Northside Road.

AMENITIES: Change room, bathroom, picnic tables, covered shelters, MobiMats.

NEARBY: The Beaches Arts and Heritage Centre (<1 kilometre), Sandy Cove Beach (2 kilometres).

EASTERN NEWFOUNDLAND

39 Sandy Cove (Eastport)

Fine white sand and relatively calm, shallow water make Sandy Cove Beach near Eastport a sought-after destination in warm weather. The beach stretches 850 metres along the bottom of a high embankment that provides protection from northern winds; the headlands on either side also offer shelter. In summer, the beach comes alive with children playing and people sunbathing, picnicking, swimming, and boating. A set of wooden stairs leads down to the beach.

An outhouse/change room, built to resemble a lighthouse, is on the hill above the beach. Just past this structure, an archway made of whale bones leads into a small park that overlooks the beach. From the park, hike the steep but short path up to Sandy Cove Lookout for a view of Newman Sound. For a longer hike, continue along the Coastal Ridge Trail for 13 kilometres to the town of Salvage.

At the west end of the beach is a large flat rock outcrop and rocks smoothed by wave action. Here, at the back of the beach near the treeline, stairs lead up to a wooden walkway that winds through the forest for 100 metres, exiting at the western end of Tom King Boulevard.

Although the outhouse/change room at Sandy Cove is wheelchair accessible, reaching the beach requires descending stairs. Visit nearby Eastport for wheelchair-accessible beaches.

COORDINATES: 48.641147, -53.729808.
DIRECTIONS: In Eastport, head east on Sandy Cove Road and turn left on Tom King Boulevard. Follow Tom King Boulevard 420 metres to Down Below Road and turn right. Park in the designated area near the end of the road on the right.
AMENITIES: Outhouse and change room, benches.
NEARBY: Crooked Tree Park with freshwater swimming pond, playground, and walking trail (<1 kilometre).

107

40 Naked Man Beach

You will probably not see any naked men at Naked Man Beach, but you may see a rock formation that resembles one. The impression is created by the rock pillars just offshore, but only when viewed from the sandbar (accessible during low tide) at the north end of the beach. From the sandbar, look north to view the Bacon Strip, a long band of red and white rock embedded in the cliff face. En route to the sandbar are a waterfall and a shallow cave dubbed the Cook House, where fishers prepared food on rainy days.

Naked Man Beach is in Plate Cove West, at the end of a 2.7-kilometre walking and ATV trail through the forest. The final kilometre of the trail is a steady descent toward the coast and is steep in sections, with loose stones.

The trail finishes at a bluff above the beach at a privately owned cabin with a white perimeter fence. Visitors are invited to enjoy the view from Hogan's Lookout and to use the picnic table and benches, but please respect the property. To access the beach, take the short path at the far end of the yard; a rope is in place to assist with the descent.

Less than 2 kilometres along the coast north of Naked Man Beach is Red Beach, named for its red granite cliffs and sand. Reach Red Beach via a 1.5-kilometre trail near the end of the main road through Plate Cove West. As of 2022, it was difficult to get down onto the beach from the trail, but plans were in place to improve access.

COORDINATES: 48.481468, -53.515929 (Naked Man trailhead); 48.498185, -53.522349 (Naked Man Beach); 48.505563, -53.508373 (Red Beach trailhead); 48.509914, -53.516670 (Red Beach).

DIRECTIONS: From the TCH, take Route 230 to Southern Bay and then Route 235 for 14 kilometres to Plate Cove West. The parking area is on the left, approximately 1 kilometre past Round Da Bay Inn.

AMENITIES: Benches, picnic table.

NEARBY: Jiggin' Head Trail (5 kilometres), Tickle Cove Sea Arch (15 kilometres), King's Cove Lighthouse Trail and Brook Point (16 kilometres).

EASTERN NEWFOUNDLAND

41 Long Beach

Beaches have been the inspiration for many songs—usually upbeat tunes about good times in the surf, sand, and sun. Long Beach in Bonavista is also believed to have inspired a song, but this one is related to a devastating event that occurred 3,500 kilometres away.

On November 1, 1755, a massive earthquake caused death and destruction in Lisbon, Portugal, and triggered a tsunami, which travelled across the ocean to Bonavista. Parts of the town became inundated with water, as recounted in the traditional song "A Great Big Sea Hove in Long Beach." An interpretive sign at the beach tells the story.

The beach is in Bayley's Cove, north of Bonavista Harbour. Its location on the west side of the Bonavista Peninsula makes it an excellent place to watch the sunset, and it is also a popular caplin-catching destination in season.

Photo © Logan MacDonald

COORDINATES: 48.656245, -53.118072.
DIRECTIONS: Follow Route 230 through Bonavista to Fitzgerald's Lane and then Long Beach Road. Park on the side of the road near one of the access points in the fencing.
AMENITIES: None.
NEARBY: O'Dea's Pond Boardwalk (<1 kilometre), Ryan Premises National Historic Site (2 kilometres), Dungeon Provincial Park (3 kilometres), Cape Bonavista Lighthouse (6 kilometres).

Archaeological evidence shows that in Bonavista, as in many parts of Newfoundland, Indigenous Peoples occupied the area long before European colonization. To reference this, as part of the 2021 Bonavista Biennale contemporary art festival, artist Logan MacDonald exhibited excerpts at the beach from John Cabot's 1497 expedition notes.

42 Sandy Cove (Elliston)

Originally called Bird Island Cove, Elliston is famous for its puffin colony: visitors can get closer to the birds by land than anywhere else in North America. It is also known as the root-cellar capital of the world, with over 130 root cellars dotting the landscape. A third reason to visit Elliston is the beautiful beach at Sandy Cove, less than 1 kilometre west of the puffin-viewing site.

As its name suggests, the beach is covered in sand, but it is also backed by a wide band of loose stones beginning near the high-tide line; the amount of sand visible at any given time depends on the tide. On fine days, the beach is a popular swimming spot, owing to its sandy bottom and relatively shallow water, and children splash in the brook at the western end. When waves are high, enjoy the beach from the shore, although surfers are occasionally spotted.

Parking is available in the unpaved lot next to the beach, and there is a takeout on site. Directly across the road, Elliston Municipal Park has bathrooms as well as serviced and unserviced campsites, some with a view of the beach. The park and beach also host popular events, including the Bird Island Puffin Festival and the Roots, Rants, and Roars culinary festival.

COORDINATES: 48.624254, -53.031564.

DIRECTIONS: From the TCH, take Route 230 toward Bonavista and then Route 238 toward Elliston. In Elliston, take Main Street or Trickem Road to Maberly Road. The beach is just over 1 kilometre down Maberly Road.

AMENITIES: Takeout with picnic tables, municipal park with bathrooms and campsites.

NEARBY: Puffin-viewing site (<1 kilometre), Sealers Memorial (1 kilometre), Dungeon Provincial Park (9 kilometres).

The seal fishery was once a part of life in Elliston, and the town lost eight men in the sealing disaster of 1914 involving the vessels *Newfoundland* and *Southern Cross*. About 1 kilometre north of the beach, a memorial honours the many Newfoundland and Labrador men who perished in the disaster.

43 Port Rexton Area

In the town of Port Rexton, Robin Hood Beach is an iconic example of the narrow, roadside pebble beaches found throughout Newfoundland. With colourful wildflowers, picnic tables, and benches, and parking adjacent to the beach, it is a convenient place to stretch your legs while exploring the area.

On either side of Robin Hood Beach, the land extends outward into headlands with opportunities to visit more scenic beaches. To the east, the 8.2-kilometre Fox Island Trail takes you around the headland to sites of interest, including an aquarium just off the trail at Champney's West and rocky beaches in Fox Bay and Outer Fox Island Cove.

To the west is the Skerwink Trail in Trinity East, which boasts a long, pebble beach at Sam White's Cove. A smaller beach is located at Devils Cove on the west side of the bay, about 2 kilometres from Robin Hood Beach.

COORDINATES: 48.394996, -53.325870 (Robin Hood Beach); 48.386587, -53.306334 (Fox Island trailhead); 48.37917, -53.34028 (Skerwink trailhead).

DIRECTIONS: From the TCH, take Route 230 to Port Rexton. Robin Hood Beach is in the middle of town off Ship Cove Road. For the beaches on the hiking trails, head to Champney's West or Trinity East and locate the trailheads.

AMENITIES: Picnic/rest area at Robin Hood Beach.

NEARBY: Gunn Hill Lookout (1 kilometre), Lockston Path Provincial Park (7 kilometres).

EASTERN NEWFOUNDLAND

44 Sam White's Cove

The beach at Sam White's Cove (also known as White Cove) is a fitting finale to the internationally renowned Skerwink Trail, located between Port Rexton and Trinity East. Voted one of the top 35 hikes in North America and Europe by *Travel & Leisure* magazine, the trail makes a 5-kilometre loop around the headland between Robinhood Bay and Trinity Harbour, offering views of cliffs, sea stacks, and the surrounding communities.

The beach, located on the western side of the loop where the trail descends to sea level, is the final opportunity to appreciate the coastal views before heading inland through a meadow and alongside Farm Pond to complete the hike. For a panoramic view of the cove and the Fort Point Lighthouse in Trinity, climb the side trail to the lookout on the eastern side of the cove before heading down to the beach.

If you wish to visit the beach without hiking the entire loop, take the path on the right from the trailhead on Rocky Hill Road. This path runs counterclockwise around the loop and reaches Sam White's Cove in about 1 kilometre.

COORDINATES: 48.37917, -53.34028 (trailhead); 48.372380, -53.339255 (Sam White's Cove).

DIRECTIONS: From the TCH, take Route 230 to Rocky Hill Road in Port Rexton and look for the Skerwink Trail sign. A parking lot is across the road.

AMENITIES: Gazebo at the trailhead on Rocky Hill Road, outhouse a short distance down the left path.

NEARBY: Fox Island Trail (5 kilometres), Lockston Path Provincial Park (8 kilometres), historic town of Trinity (10 kilometres), Fort Point Lighthouse (16 kilometres).

EASTERN NEWFOUNDLAND

45 Heart's Ease Beach

Heart's Ease Beach in Gooseberry Cove, Trinity Bay, has attracted hunters and fishers for thousands of years. Today, it is a destination for hikers, birdwatchers, and nature lovers.

The cobblestone beach, sprinkled with driftwood and the skeletons of fish and sea urchins, is easily accessed by a 200-metre hike down Jimmy Dick's Path. Take the walking path, indicated by a sign, and not the ATV trail. The wooded path is well maintained with boardwalks over marshy spots and ropes to assist with steeper sections. An outhouse and set of swings are also available along the trail. As you near the beach, take a short detour on the right to Ian's Lookout, where you can sit on a bench and enjoy the panoramic view. Down on the beach, two picnic tables provide a place to enjoy a mug-up.

The tombolo beach connects the mainland to Heart's Ease Island, which has a 1-kilometre-long path winding around its perimeter. This trail is rougher than Jimmy Dick's Path—because the ground is uneven, use caution when hiking near the cliffs. A special treat is the sea arch on the eastern side of the island.

Another path, called Jack Baker's Hill, is also accessible from the trailhead in the parking lot. This trail leads to Gooseberry Cove Lookout for more stunning views. Don't forget to sign the guestbook at the trailhead on your way out.

COORDINATES: 48.036906, -53.634757 (trailhead); 48.034571, -53.629536 (beach).
DIRECTIONS: From the TCH, take Route 204 (Main Road) to Gooseberry Cove Road. Follow this road to St. Alban the Martyr Anglican Church and park in the unpaved lot behind the church. The trailhead is at the end of the parking lot on the right.
AMENITIES: Picnic tables on beach, outhouse on trail.
NEARBY: West Random Head Trail (<1 kilometre); boat basin, recreation area, and rocky beach in the community of Long Beach (17 kilometres).

EASTERN NEWFOUNDLAND

46 Terrenceville Beach

An early name for Terrenceville was Fortune Bay Bottom because of its location at the end of a long, narrow arm in the northeast corner of the bay. The sand and pebble beach is on a long spit that almost entirely separates the end of the arm from the ocean, creating a large barachois.

More than 1 kilometre across at its widest point and covered in grass and wildflowers, the spit is locally referred to as the Meadow. The space was used by migratory fishers and early settlers to dry fish and plant vegetable gardens. These days, the Bottom of the Bay Trail, a 1-kilometre-long gravel path, offers views of the bay, barachois, and surrounding hills. A gazebo and picnic table make it a fine place for a picnic, and benches are provided along the trail.

Because it is at the bottom (or head) of Fortune Bay, the beach tends to be the final landing place for marine debris from the region. The community holds periodic beach cleanups, but visitors who want to spend time along the water's edge or go for a dip may prefer to do so in the barachois, which also has a beachy shoreline. The barachois is also popular with kayakers and birdwatchers.

COORDINATES: 47.667888, -54.724235.
DIRECTIONS: From the Burin Peninsula Highway (Route 210), take Route 211 and then Main Drive into Terrenceville. Follow Barasway Drive down to the beach and park in one of the cleared areas in the Meadow.
AMENITIES: Benches, gazebo, picnic table.
NEARBY: Sunset Falls (3 kilometres), freshwater swimming below the highway bridge at South East Brook Waterfall (7 kilometres).

EASTERN NEWFOUNDLAND

47 Broad Cove Beach

Broad Cove Beach is best known for a single tree clinging tenaciously to a sea stack, dubbed the Friar, but this is not its only interesting feature. Outcroppings of heavily veined granite occur along the high banks. At the far end of the beach, a "mousehole" at the base of the cliff creates a small window through the rock, although for the best view you must wade into the water. The beach is also a popular place to have a picnic or campfire or to search for sea glass among the pebbles.

Broad Cove Beach is located on Route 212 between Little Harbour East and Harbour Mille, in a small inlet of Fortune Bay. Sections of the coastal drive around the inlet to the beach are stunning, with the water on one side and the towering Hare Hills on the other. Parking at the beach is limited, but there is space for a few cars to pull off the road.

Across the highway from the beach, a gravel road leads up the hill to a cemetery. From there, you can hike to a more secluded beach at Brook Cove, about 500 metres west. Harbour Mille also has a small, rocky beach at the south end of the community.

COORDINATES: 47.590754, -54.864033.

DIRECTIONS: From the TCH, take Route 210 and then Route 212 toward St. Bernard's-Jacques Fontaine. At Jacques Fontaine, turn right and continue toward Harbour Mille-Little Harbour East. Broad Cove Beach is just past Little Harbour East.

AMENITIES: Picnic tables.

NEARBY: Mille Harbour Lookout Trail (2 kilometres), Berry Hill Trail in Bay L'Argent (15 kilometres).

EASTERN NEWFOUNDLAND

48 Frenchman's Cove

Frenchman's Cove is on Route 213, or the "Beaches and Barasway Loop." The loop leaves the main highway between Marystown and Grand Bank and runs for 14 kilometres between Frenchman's Cove and Garnish, passing by several beaches.

Travelling from west to east, you first encounter Frenchman's Cove Viewpark, which offers interpretive panels and a wheelchair-accessible platform overlooking a long, pebble beach. Continuing east from the Viewpark, as you enter Frenchman's Cove a building resembling a small lighthouse is on the left. This is the site of an airstrip built alongside the beach in the 1950s. To access the beach, follow the path to the left of the chain-link fence.

Near the east end of the community is Frenchman's Cove Provincial Park, developed in the 1960s on the shores of Frenchman's Cove Barasway. Across the road from the park, a beach stretches for 2 kilometres to Garnish, with the ocean on one side and the barachois on the other. The beach is a popular spot to watch the sunset or beachcomb, while the barachois offers opportunities to spot birds, including the endangered red knot. In Garnish, head inland on Sunset Drive to return to the main highway and complete the loop.

COORDINATES: 47.194669, -55.433876 (Viewpark); 47.210584, -55.415789 (beach at airstrip); 47.217266, -55.400298 (beach across from provincial park).

DIRECTIONS: From Grand Bank, continue east on Route 220 and turn left onto Route 213 to enter the western portion of the loop. Alternatively, from Marystown, take Columbia Drive and Route 210, then turn right onto Route 213 to enter the eastern portion of the loop.

AMENITIES: Benches and picnic tables at the Viewpark, further amenities at the provincial park (day-use fee required).

NEARBY*: Long Ridge Hiking Trail (3 kilometres), Garnish-Point Rosie Trail (6 kilometres).
*Approximate distances from Frenchman's Cove Provincial Park.

The beaches along the Beaches and Barasway Loop are composed mostly of pebbles. For a smaller but sandy beach, take the gravel road about 700 metres before the turnoff onto Route 213 toward the Viewpark.

49 Golden Sands

Golden Sands Resort is a privately owned park and campground on a large freshwater pond, about a 10-minute drive from Marystown. On the northwest shore of the lake is the long, golden-brown sandy beach for which the resort is named.

The water is shallow near the shore but deepens farther out, making it ideal for both swimming and boating. Be aware, however, that there are no lifeguards. As the sand is mixed with tiny pebbles and can be rough underfoot, bring sandals for long walks on the beach.

The family-friendly resort offers miniature golf, a playground, and a trackless train. Full-service RV sites, tent sites, and cabins—including pet-friendly and wheelchair-accessible ones—are available for rent. There is a day-use fee.

Golden Sands is conveniently situated for exploring Route 220, which follows the coast in a loop around the tip of the Burin Peninsula. From the resort, turn left on Winterland Road (Route 222) to reach the north side of the loop toward Frenchman's Cove Provincial Park, Grand Bank, and the Fortune Head Ecological Reserve. Alternatively, turn right on Winterland Road to reach the south side of the loop toward Burin, the Chambers Cove Trail in St. Lawrence, and a long sandy beach at Point au Gaul.

COORDINATES: 47.128528, -55.267136 (entrance to park on Winterland Road); 47.117301, -55.276092 (beach).

DIRECTIONS: Take Route 210 through Marystown, turning right at Columbia Drive. At Winterland Road (Route 222), turn left and drive 4 kilometres until you see signs for the Golden Sands Resort. Follow the gravel road approximately 1 kilometre to the resort.

AMENITIES: Full-service campsites, dumping station, cabin and boat rentals, bathrooms, showers, laundry, restaurant, canteen.

NEARBY: Winterland Ecomuseum and Trail (5 kilometres), Salt Pond Walking Trail (8 kilometres), Landing Place Pond Walking Trail and Swimming Area (13 kilometres), Cooks Lookout Trail (16 kilometres).

50 Shoal Cove

Nestled between two headlands on the south shore of the Burin Peninsula, and within easy driving distance of St. Lawrence, the beach at Shoal Cove is a popular destination for rest and recreation. Its soft, fine sand is perfect for sandcastle building, sunbathing, or picnicking, and children enjoy splashing in the pooling water from the brook that runs down from Shoal Pond to the beach. Many people come to watch the incredible wave action, which also attracts surfers. If you venture into the ocean, however, be cautious: signs warn of a strong undertow and swimming is not supervised.

The hills surrounding the beach offer opportunities for berry picking, ATV riding, and hiking. On the east side of the beach, a rough ATV/hiking trail runs up the hill and along the coast for over 2 kilometres to Ferryland Head. On the west side, just off the tip of the headland, is a rocky island called Hares Ears. The headland offers a view of Shoal Cove as well as Salt Cove to the west.

Two coves west of Shoal Cove is Chambers Cove, an important historical landmark. In 1942, residents of the area undertook the daring rescue of nearly 200 sailors from US Navy ships that had run aground at Chambers Cove and nearby Lawn Point during a storm.

From Chambers Cove, you can follow an undeveloped trail along the coastline all the way to Lawn. A network of gravel roads, many leading to mines that once operated in the area, now permit access to Shoal Cove, Hares Ears, Ferryland Head, and Chambers Cove Trail.

COORDINATES: 46.883161, -55.400284.
DIRECTIONS: In St. Lawrence, drive to the end of Laurentian Avenue and turn right onto Pollux Crescent, which later becomes Iron Spring Road. After 2.6 kilometres, take a left, followed soon by another left to head down to the beach, where parking is available. The total distance is 3.6 kilometres on the gravel road, but signage is good and the road is usually well maintained.
AMENITIES: Bench.
NEARBY: Chambers Cove Trail (2 kilometres), Cape Chapeau Rouge Trail (3 kilometres), St. Lawrence Miners Memorial Museum (6 kilometres).

EASTERN NEWFOUNDLAND

51 Backcove Beach

When travelling around the Burin Peninsula, stretch your legs at Backcove Beach in Lawn. Conveniently located next to the highway, the small sandy beach lies midway between two other sandy beaches at St. Lawrence and Lord's Cove that are larger but off the beaten track.

Backcove Beach is situated in Great Lawn Harbour. As with all Newfoundland outports, the fishery played an important role in Lawn's history, and the community lost its share of lives to the sea. Dedicated to their memory, a lookout on the hill next to the beach offers a view through the harbour toward the open ocean. At the east end of the beach, a narrow channel provides passage into the protected end of the harbour. Visitors interested in viewing boats may find some docked at the wharves north of the beach.

For those who wish to explore farther afield, Little Lawn Harbour, east of Lawn, has a long barachois beach covered in pink pebbles, but getting there takes some effort. The beach is nearly 5 kilometres down a narrow, unmaintained gravel road that is more appropriate for ATVs and hikers than cars. The road begins behind the graveyard near the old water tower, on the southeast side of the harbour.

COORDINATES: 46.942697, -55.542430.
DIRECTIONS: From the TCH, take Route 210 and then Route 220 into Lawn. At the end of town, take a left at the sign for the Harbour Authority. Park in the large gravel lot next to the beach.
AMENITIES: Benches, picnic table, RV park, takeout on site.
NEARBY: Lawn Heritage Museum (<1 kilometre), Sandy Cove Beach (9 kilometres), Chambers Cove (18 kilometres).

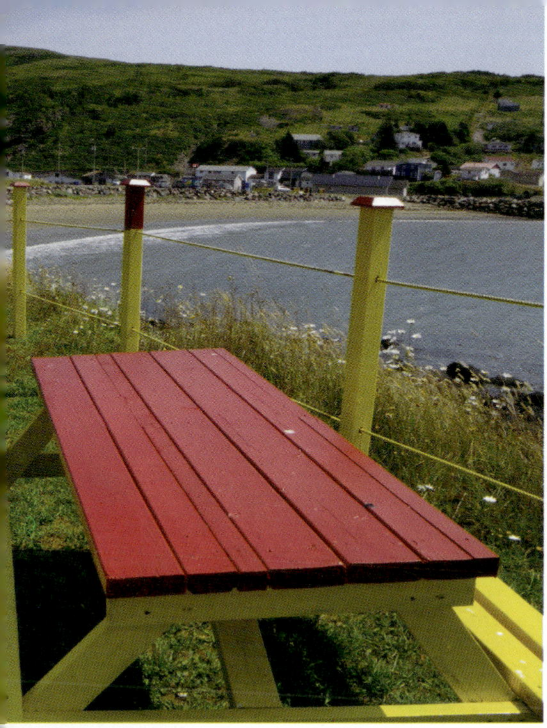

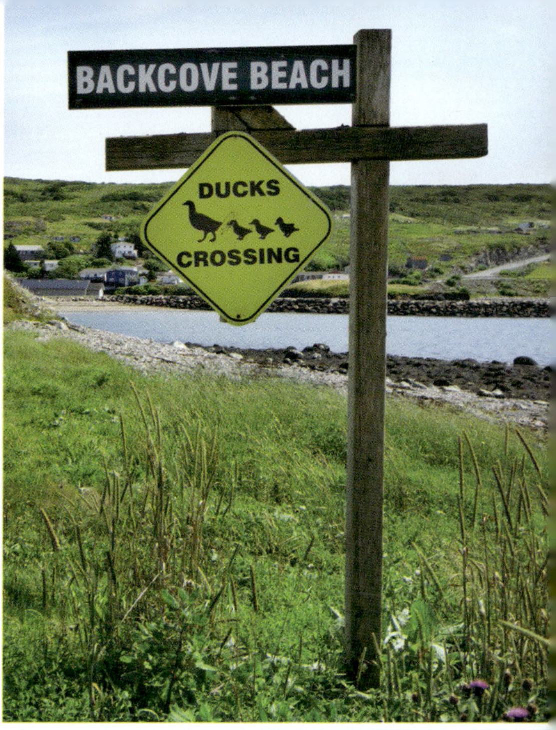

131

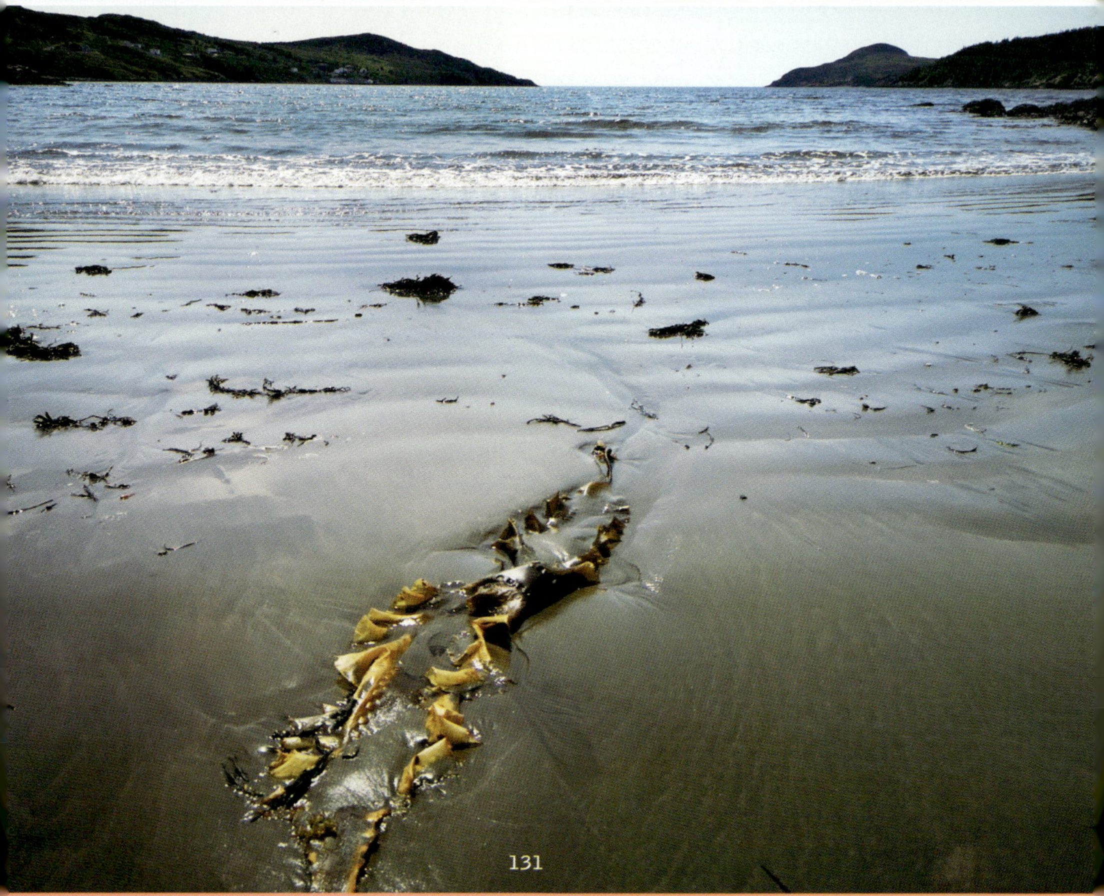

Sandy Cove (Lord's Cove)

As some of the locals like to say, "You take the turn, and the view takes your breath." The turn refers to a curve in the road toward Sandy Cove that leads to the stunning beach surrounded by rolling hills and grass-covered fields.

The houses that were once at the cove are gone, but the beach is still a gathering spot for residents of Lord's Cove and surrounding communities. People come to enjoy the sand and waves, have a campfire or boil-up on the beach, pick berries, hike along the headlands, or tour the area on ATVs. The annual Sandy Cove Family Fun Day attracts crowds each summer, with food, entertainment, and games. Visitors from beyond the local area are discovering the beach, and surfers have even come from Hawaii to ride the waves.

As with anywhere else in Newfoundland, the ocean at Sandy Cove is often quite cold, and swimming alone is not recommended due to hidden currents and undertows. The winding stream that flows from Sandy Cove Pond to the ocean on the western side of the beach provides a safer, and warmer, place for children to splash.

A committee of local volunteers has

provided amenities for beachgoers, including change rooms, outhouses, benches, picnic tables, and firepits. Tent and RV camping is permitted, but there are no services. Regular maintenance keeps the 5-kilometre gravel road to the beach passable for vehicles, but it can still be rough at times, depending on recent weather.

EASTERN NEWFOUNDLAND

COORDINATES: 46.898566, -55.617050.

DIRECTIONS: From the TCH, take Route 210 to Marystown and then Route 220 for approximately 65 kilometres to Lord's Cove. Just as you enter Lord's Cove, make a sharp left onto Back Road and follow it to the beach (the last 5 kilometres are unpaved). Do not try to access Sandy Cove by vehicle via Old Lord's Cove Road near Lawn, as that unmaintained road is very rough.

AMENITIES: Outhouses, change rooms, benches, picnic tables, firepits.

NEARBY: Wave Energy Research Centre (6 kilometres), Backcove Beach (13 kilometres), Point au Gaul Stand (15 kilometres).

A collection of small offshore islands visible from Sandy Cove make up the Lawn Bay Ecological Reserve, including Middle Lawn Island, Swale Island, and Colombier Island. The reserve supports the only known colony of Manx shearwater in North America, a sizable colony of Leach's storm petrels, and other seabird species. Access to the islands is restricted during the breeding season from mid-March to late October, and boaters must keep a distance of at least 100 metres to avoid disturbing the birds.

Photo © Martine Blue

53 Point au Gaul Strand

Point au Gaul is near the southerly tip of the Burin Peninsula in Lamaline Bay, east of Lamaline. The name Lamaline is thought to be a corruption of the French *la maligne*, meaning malignant or malicious, because of the numerous dangerous shoals and rocks in the bay.

The landscape in the area is generally flat and covered in low shrubs and grass, which leaves the beach (which local residents call the Strand) exposed to the elements. In fine weather, however, it is a wonderful place to relax, walk, or play in the fine grey sand. Watch the shorebirds, search for sand dollars, or create designs with the many pebbles scattered throughout the sand.

At the northwest end of the beach, large boulders have been painted by local artists to resemble quilts and Jellybean Row houses. Across the road is Frenchman's Pond, a swimming area with colourful change rooms and picnic tables. The beach does not have an official campground or facilities, but RVs sometimes park on the grassy areas next to the Strand.

Point au Gaul was affected greatly by the tidal wave that struck the Burin Peninsula in 1929. Of the 27 people who perished, nine were from Point au Gaul, and almost every home in the community was destroyed or damaged. Learn more about the tragedy at the museum in the nearby town of Lamaline.

COORDINATES: 46.868151, -55.761011.

DIRECTIONS: From the TCH, take Route 210 and then Route 220 to Point au Gaul. At Point au Gaul, look for the "Park-Strand" sign. There is a parking area adjacent to the beach.

AMENITIES: Picnic tables and change rooms at Frenchman's Pond across from the beach.

NEARBY: Lamaline Heritage Museum (3 kilometres), Allan's Island Lighthouse (7 kilometres), beaches at Taylor's Bay (5 kilometres) and Point May (15 kilometres).

EASTERN NEWFOUNDLAND

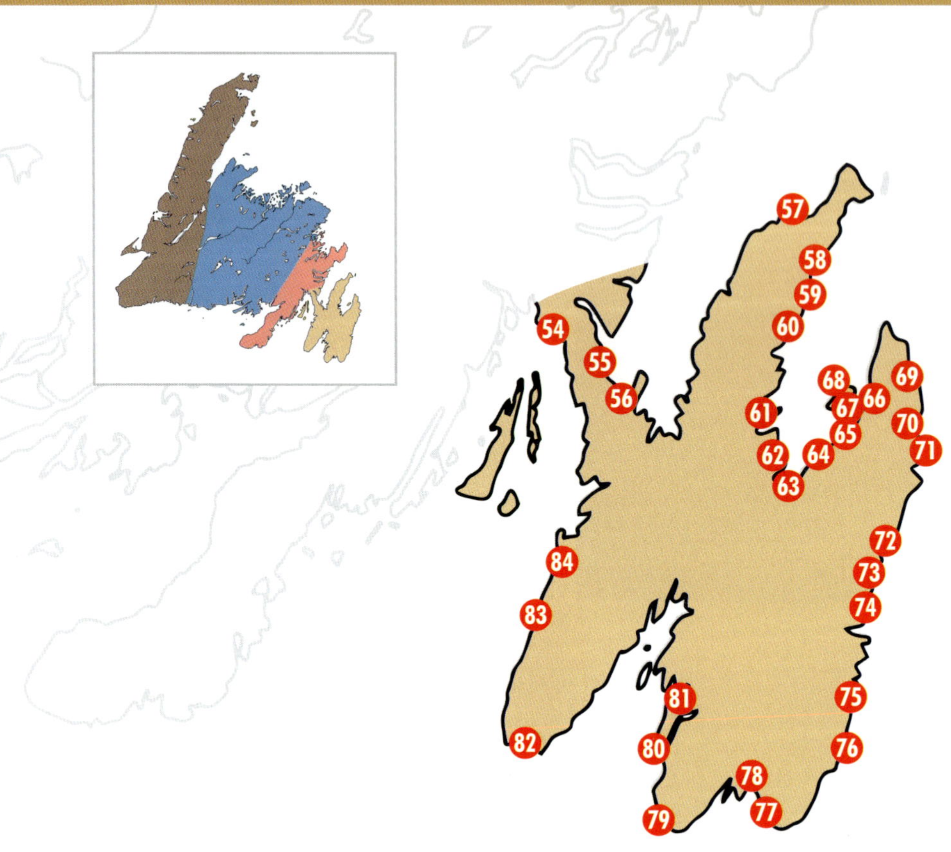

54	Arnold's Cove	70	Middle Cove
55	Chance Cove	71	Outer Cove
56	Bellevue Beach	72	Ragged Beach
57	Goods Beach	73	Mobile Beach
58	Northern Bay Sands	74	Tors Cove Beach
59	Southern Beach	75	Ferryland Beach
60	Salmon Cove Sands	76	Cappahayden Beach
61	Three Sisters Beach	77	Portugal Cove South
62	The Tide	78	Biscay Bay
63	Holyrood Beach	79	St. Shott's Beach
64	Manuel's Beach	80	St. Vincent's Beach
65	Topsail Beach	81	Gulch Beach
66	Beachy Cove	82	Point Lance Sands
67	Lance Cove	83	Gooseberry Cove
68	Grebe's Nest	84	Great Beach
69	Torbay Beach		

Avalon Peninsula & Isthmus of Avalon

The most easterly part of Newfoundland is the Avalon Peninsula, including the 50-kilometre-long isthmus that connects the peninsula to the main body of the island. With four major bays and hundreds of coves, the Avalon is home to dozens of beaches, all of them within a few hours' drive of St. John's, the provincial capital.

Most of the beaches are rocky, in keeping with the Avalon's rugged coastline, although it is possible to find beaches covered in soft, fine sand. Salmon Cove Sands and Northern Bay Sands lie along a scenic route called the Baccalieu Trail, which loops around the peninsula between Trinity Bay and Conception Bay North. In Conception Bay South and in the areas north of St. John's, beaches are typically composed of cobbles and pebbles, with some coarse dark sand.

They are still popular destinations: the beaches in Holyrood, Topsail, and Middle Cove are some of the most frequented on the island.

South of St. John's is the Irish Loop, named for the primary heritage of those who live in the region. Usually driven from east to west, the route winds around the southeastern portion of the Avalon for more than 300 kilometres. The initial portion follows Route 10 south from St. John's along the eastern edge of the Avalon, known as the Southern Shore. A string of rocky beaches is easily accessible from roads within the communities dotting the coastline.

Additional beaches can be accessed from the East Coast Trail, a 336-kilometre network of hiking paths that extends all the way south to Cappahayden. Two

of the best hikes for beach lovers are Beaches Path from Witless Bay to Mobile, and Tinkers Point Path from Mobile to Tors Cove. Visible from these trails is the Witless Bay Ecological Reserve, a cluster of four offshore islands that hosts the largest Atlantic puffin colony in North America and the second-largest Leach's storm petrel colony in the world.

History enthusiasts may be interested in some of the beaches farther down the shore. At Ferryland, archaeologists have uncovered one of the oldest English colonial settlements in Newfoundland.

At Cappahayden, a beachside memorial recounts the wreck of the *Florizel*, a luxury passenger liner which ran aground there in 1918.

South of Cappahayden, Route 10 veers westward across mostly uninhabited inland barrens for more than 30 kilometres to Trepassey Bay. En route is a long pebble beach at Chance Cove Provincial Park (not to be confused with Chance Cove in Trinity Bay). Be aware, however, that getting there involves a 6-kilometre drive over a rough dirt road through the park.

A major feature of interest in Trepassey Bay is Mistaken Point Ecological Reserve. Situated along the road to Cape Race in Portugal Cove South, the reserve holds some of the oldest and best-preserved fossils in the world. Beaches in the area offer scenic places to relax and imagine what the Earth was like when these organisms existed 580 million years ago.

From Portugal Cove South, Route 10 proceeds west through Trepassey Bay before crossing the barrens to St. Mary's Bay. Look for whales at St. Vincent's Beach—this is one of the best places in Newfoundland to view humpbacks from land. At St. Vincent's, Route 10 becomes Route 90 and heads north toward the TCH, with another beach and coastal hiking trail in Point La Haye.

To explore beyond the Irish Loop, take Route 91 in St. Catherine's and then Route 92 South at Colinet for a scenic drive around the southwest section of the Avalon. The highway runs south down St. Mary's Bay, around the cape, and then north up into Placentia Bay along the Cape Shore. The total distance is 120 kilometres from Colinet to the town of Placentia, with scattered small communities and scarce amenities (be sure you have enough gas).

At Cape St. Mary's, a road leads out to an ecological reserve where visitors can watch thousands of birds swoop and soar

around a towering sea stack that stands remarkably close to the shore. Some of the Avalon's rare sandy beaches occur along the Cape Shore, most notably at Point Lance and Gooseberry Cove.

The northernmost part of the route is at Placentia, the French capital of Newfoundland until the British took control of the area in 1713. Visitors can view the remains of fortifications at Castle Hill National Historic Site, which has an unimpeded view of the town's long, cobble beach. From Placentia, Route 91 to Colinet completes the loop but is unpaved for 24 kilometres. Alternatively, Route 100 connects Placentia with the TCH near Whitbourne and is a smoother ride.

54 Arnold's Cove

The scalloped shoreline of Arnold's Cove is punctuated by a series of smaller coves with pebble beaches. Passing through many of these beaches is the Bordeaux Trail. Rated as easy to moderate, the hiking trail has no significant changes in elevation but is lengthy at 12 kilometres return (skip the side trails for a 9-kilometre hike).

From the trailhead in the parking area, a gravel path leads to the first beach. Take time to explore before heading right along the Bordeaux Trail, which follows the western shore of the cove. Portions of the trail pass through forest but much of it crosses grassy headlands and beaches, offering views of Placentia Bay. Merasheen (the longest island in the bay) and Long Island are visible.

Beachcombers will enjoy searching for driftwood and shells on the trail's beaches, including at Wreck Cove, Labours Cove, and Wild Cove. Near the end of the hike in the location of Adam's Head, the beaches border Bordeaux Pond and have superb views of the pond on one side and the bay on the other. A half-buried skiff is an interesting photograph opportunity.

COORDINATES:	47.763127, -53.996935 (parking lot and trailhead).
DIRECTIONS:	From the TCH, take Exit 26A to Main Road in Arnold's Cove and watch for signs for the Bordeaux Trail, located at the end of Harbour View Avenue.
AMENITIES:	Limited seating on the trail.
NEARBY:	Arnold's Cove Bird Sanctuary (2 kilometres), Drake Heritage House Museum (2 kilometres), Placentia Bay Lookout (2 kilometres).

On the southeast side of Arnold's Cove at the end of Peach Street, a 1-kilometre-return trail leads out to Otter Rub Head Lookout. Take the stairs down to a small pocket beach and sea arch. The trail is called The War Path, in reference to the anti-aircraft units and watch towers set up there by the US Military during World War II.

AVALON PENINSULA & ISTHMUS OF AVALON

55 Chance Cove

Chance Cove is approximately halfway across the isthmus of the Avalon Peninsula in Trinity Bay and should not be confused with Chance Cove Provincial Park on the southeast Avalon. Beside the main road running through the town of Chance Cove is a 700-metre-long barachois beach composed of pebbles, cobbles, and coarse grey sand.

Ample parking and a picnic area are at the western end of the beach, just off the main road. Sit and view Trinity Bay from the north side of the beach or watch the gulls that gather on the south side where the beach borders Chance Cove Pond.

At the eastern end of the beach, a hiking trail winds around the wooded headland and includes two smaller beaches, at Big Cove and Island Cove. This is a section of the 3.7-kilometre Chance Cove Coastal Trail, which begins near the Salvation Army cemetery in town. Big Cove Beach is backed by high cliffs and accessing the beach can be challenging as the path down is quite steep. A rope has been installed to assist with the descent, but many visitors still find it daunting. The beach can also be appreciated from atop the cliffs via various scenic lookouts with benches. Island Cove Beach has a wooden stairway for easier access. In 2022, plans were in place to install stairs at Big Cove.

COORDINATES: 47.673185, -53.814729 (Chance Cove Beach); 47.666772, -53.812797 (trailhead near the cemetery).

DIRECTIONS: From the TCH, take Route 201. Turn left onto Main Road (Route 16) and follow it for 7.5 kilometres to Chance Cove Beach. To reach Big Cove and Island Cove, join the coastal trail at the far end of the beach, or begin the hike at the trailhead in town.

AMENITIES: Picnic area, benches on the coastal trail.

NEARBY: Bellevue Beach (5 kilometres).

AVALON PENINSULA & ISTHMUS OF AVALON

56 Bellevue Beach

Just over an hour's drive from St. John's, Bellevue Beach Park is a popular summer destination for campers, kayakers, boaters, hikers, birdwatchers, and beach enthusiasts. While the campground has been privatized, the rest of the park, including the beach, retains status as a provincial park reserve to protect its natural features.

The long stretch of sand, pebbles, and cobbles forms a bar separating the waters of Trinity Bay from Broad Lake. Many of the campsites are adjacent to the beach or along the top of the cliffs overlooking the bay; others are tucked into the northwest corner of Broad Lake, where a pebble shoreline borders a freshwater swimming area.

Walk to the western end of the beach for a close-up view of the cliffs and sea stack. Head in the opposite direction to hike the Vinland Trail out to the narrow channel where the lake empties into the ocean. The bar widens considerably about two-thirds of the way along the beach and morphs into a landscape of low trees, lagoons, and salt marshes. The 6-kilometre (return) walk provides opportunities for birdwatching, hunting for shells and driftwood, and enjoying views of the ocean on one side and lake on the other.

COORDINATES: 47.636568, -53.777803.
DIRECTIONS: From the TCH, follow Route 201 to Main Road then turn left and look for the sign for Bellevue Beach Park. Park in the large gravel lot adjacent to the beach.
AMENITIES: Outhouses, picnic tables, semi-serviced campsites.
NEARBY: Chance Cove Beach and Coastal Hiking Trail (5 kilometres), rocky beach in the town of Bellevue (10 kilometres).

AVALON PENINSULA & ISTHMUS OF AVALON

57 Goods Beach

With the exception of those who live in New Melbourne and surrounding communities on the Bay de Verde Peninsula, most Newfoundlanders have likely never heard of Goods Beach—unless they are surfers. Known for having some of the best surfing conditions on the island, the beach attracts people interested in riding the waves well into the fall.

Calm-water days also occur at Goods Beach, when the only waves encountered are the small, low variety surfers refer to as ankle biters. Those days are perfect for walking the shoreline, hunting for shells among the rocks, or climbing on the boulders at the south end of the beach. Picnickers are welcome but open fires are not permitted.

The beach is directly across from St. Stephen's United Cemetery on Salvage Point Road. A gravel clearing adjacent to the beach provides parking and plenty of room to unload surfboards. There are

no amenities at the beach and scarce amenities in the surrounding area, but a few stores and restaurants can be found 15 kilometres east in Old Perlican.

COORDINATES: 48.049462, -53.155625.
DIRECTIONS: From the TCH near Whitbourne, take Exit 28 and follow Route 80 for approximately 88 kilometres to New Melbourne. At the mailbox shelter, turn left onto Buttons Road (which is unpaved) and drive another 350 metres to the beach.
AMENITIES: None.
NEARBY: Willow Tree Museum (10 kilometres), Hant's Harbour Lighthouse (11 kilometres), Wooden Boat Museum in Winterton (18 kilometres), pebble beach at Caplin Cove (20 kilometres).

Photo © Alexandra Noseworthy

AVALON PENINSULA & ISTHMUS OF AVALON

58 Northern Bay Sands

Like many beaches in Newfoundland, the beach at Northern Bay was used historically as a convenient place to salt and dry cod. Today, the large sandy beach is a popular destination for visitors seeking fun and relaxation.

The beach is in a privately owned park and campground, with serviced sites located next to the beach and on the forested hill above the beach. At the north end of the beach, a brook runs down the hill, creating waterfalls and freshwater pools that are popular swimming spots for children. If the tide makes it difficult to reach this area from the beach, it can be accessed by walking through the campground above the beach.

Day-use fees vary for cars, motorcycles, and walk-ins. Dogs are allowed in the park, but they are not permitted on the sand. Dogs are allowed on the beach at Salmon Cove Sands, 34 kilometres south, but there is no camping at that location. Public beaches can also be found in some other communities between Salmon Cove and Northern Bay, such as Southern Beach in Western Bay.

COORDINATES: 47.935853, -53.078838.

DIRECTIONS: From the TCH, take Route 75 and then Route 70 toward Bay de Verde. Watch for the sign for Northern Bay Sands on Route 70.

AMENITIES: Food stand, outhouses, change rooms, showers, serviced campsites with firepits and picnic tables.

NEARBY: Mouse Hole Arch (5 kilometres); beach, falls, and boardwalk at Western Bay (8 kilometres); Spout Cove Beach (16 kilometres).

59 Southern Beach

Tucked away at the end of a residential street in Western Bay, Southern Beach is less well known than some other beaches in Conception Bay North. The beach is covered with soft, grey sand backed by mixed pebbles and cobblestones. Beyond the stones, Island Pond Brook winds through a large meadow before crossing the beach to the ocean.

At the top of the path to the beach is a picnic table and small parking area. Dogs are welcome on the beach. Not far from the beach are further attractions to explore. The Western Bay Overfalls, less than 1 kilometre away off Riverhead Road, is a popular swimming spot with a small change room in the parking area.

About 1 kilometre in the opposite direction is the Western Bay Boardwalk. The boardwalk begins on Bradley's Cove Road and follows the headland on the south side of the cove for 1.4 kilometres to an automated lighthouse. Much of the boardwalk has been painted with colourful scenes and messages by community members. A collection of white crosses marks the location of a 17th-century cemetery.

COORDINATES: 47.882600, -53.080878 (road to beach); 47.885495, -53.087765 (road to falls); 47.883654, -53.070431 (boardwalk).

DIRECTIONS: The easiest access to the beach is via Southside Road (previously Roses Road), off Route 70 in Western Bay. Where Southside Road curves is a short gravel road. Pull in and walk to the beach (about 100 metres), or drive to the small parking area above the beach.

AMENITIES: Picnic table, change room at Western Bay Overfalls.

NEARBY: Western Bay Overfalls (<1 kilometre), Western Bay Boardwalk (1 kilometre), Northern Bay Sands (8 kilometres), Salmon Cove Sands (16 kilometres).

153

AVALON PENINSULA & ISTHMUS OF AVALON

60 Salmon Cove Sands

Salmon Cove Sands attracts visitors with its plentiful amenities and natural beauty. Soft sand invites you to walk barefoot along the shoreline, and the boulders in the middle of the cove create a dramatic backdrop for photographs.

The beach offers ample room to throw a frisbee, challenge friends to a game of volleyball, or erect a sun shelter and drift off to the sound of the waves. Pets are allowed on the beach but must be kept on leash. Camping is not permitted.

Children can swim in the relatively warm water of the Salmon Cove River, which enters the cove at the north end of the beach. Use caution when swimming in the cove itself, especially when the sea is rough, as the currents can be quite strong.

A network of wheelchair-accessible boardwalks is located on the grassy area behind the beach. At various points along the boardwalks are change rooms, outhouses, a picnic area, and a small shop selling beach supplies, souvenirs, and hot and cold snacks. An accessible observation deck with benches overlooks the beach.

On the south side of the cove near the park entrance, take the Trail of the Eagles to a lookout atop the cliffs and see if you can spot the majestic birds.

COORDINATES: 47.783025, -53.157474.

DIRECTIONS: From the TCH, take Route 75 to Route 70. In Salmon Cove, turn right on Beach Avenue at the sign for Salmon Cove Sands. A large unpaved lot adjacent to the beach provides plenty of parking.

AMENITIES: Outhouses, change rooms, picnic area, canteen.

NEARBY: Trail of the Eagles (<1 kilometre), Shades of the Past Museum (4 kilometres), Harbour Rock Hill Park (12 kilometres), Southern Beach (16 kilometres).

AVALON PENINSULA & ISTHMUS OF AVALON

61 Three Sisters Beach

On the south shore of Spaniard's Bay Harbour, huddled together as if engaged in conversation, are the sea stacks known as the Three Sisters. The stacks are the main attraction on the small shingle beach that surrounds them, drawing visitors down the stairs from the bluff above. Parking is available in a pullout about 200 metres beyond the beach access.

The beach is a popular site for family outings and community events, including the annual caplin roll in early summer, as the fish wash up there in large numbers. Low tide is the best time to visit as the retreating water widens the beach and allows for closer access to the rock formations.

Three Sisters Beach is accessible by car on a gravel road that forms part of the Bay Roberts Shoreline Heritage Walk, also called the Mad Rock Trail. Beginning on Water Street in Bay Roberts East, the trail meanders through grassy meadows, over rock outcroppings, and along roadways for approximately 8 kilometres. .

COORDINATES: 47.619925, -53.210392.

DIRECTIONS: In the town of Bay Roberts, follow Water Street for 7 kilometres to the end of the pavement. The stairs to the beach are approximately 400 metres down the gravel road on the left.

AMENITIES: Picnic table on the road above beach; benches, outhouses, and picnic tables along the hiking trail.

NEARBY: Hibb's Hole Fisherman's Museum (17 kilometres), Green Point Lighthouse (17 kilometres), *Kyle* shipwreck (18 kilometres).

AVALON PENINSULA & ISTHMUS OF AVALON

62 The Tide

The Tide is a small gravel beach and swimming pond in Harbour Main, just off the Conception Bay Highway. Maloney's River empties into the harbour at the spot, with a waterfall running under the highway bridge and into the pond.

Shallow and well maintained, The Tide is a popular destination for local families looking to cool off on hot summer days. Although there is no lifeguard on duty, life preservers are provided. Picnic tables and barbecues line the beach, and a bathroom with running water is in the parking area, about 100 metres east of the site.

To access the swimming area, follow the wooden walkway running alongside the beach from the parking area. Alternatively, take the staircase just west of the highway bridge on the Conception Bay Highway. A paved pathway east of the highway bridge makes the site accessible to visitors with wheelchairs, walkers, or strollers.

For those looking for a quieter beach experience, the nearby town of Chapel's Cove has a long, cobble beach with picnic tables and barbecues, although the cold ocean water makes that beach less amenable to swimming.

COORDINATES: 47.431727, -53.158381 (parking area); 47.432141, -53.159626 (beach).
DIRECTIONS: From the TCH, take Route 62 or 63 to Route 60 (Conception Bay Highway) in Harbour Main. Look for the sign for The Tide between Hickey's Road and the Rising Tide Convenience Store. The parking area is about 100 metres east of the beach on Route 60.
AMENITIES: Bathroom, picnic tables, benches, barbecues.
NEARBY: Avondale Railway Museum (5 kilometres), Holyrood Beach (8 kilometres), Conception Harbour shipwreck (8 kilometres), Conception Harbour Overfalls (9 kilometres).

AVALON PENINSULA & ISTHMUS OF AVALON

63 Holyrood Beach

Holyrood Beach (sometimes called Main Beach) is a long cobble beach in the South Arm of Holyrood Bay. Until the mid-1900s, trains travelled back and forth along the top of the beach, transporting passengers between the town and other communities. Today, a boardwalk has replaced the track and become a highlight of the town.

The boardwalk includes ramps, ample space for mobility devices, and a wheelchair-accessible picnic area at the boardwalk's western end. Parking is directly in front of the boardwalk and beach.

Learn about the history of Holyrood from interpretive signs installed along the boardwalk, or relax on a bench and watch the boats come and go from the Holyrood Marina and Terra Nova Yacht Club on the east side of the bay. On the west side of the bay is the Holyrood Marine Base, a world-class ocean research and training centre.

If you decide to venture down onto the cobble beach for some beachcombing or a dip in the water, look both ways before stepping off the boardwalk, as an ATV path runs along the top of the beach. The ATV trail and boardwalk are part of T'Railway Provincial Park, which extends across the island on the old railway bed.

COORDINATES: 47.385659, -53.132736.
DIRECTIONS: From the TCH, take Holyrood Access Road (Route 62) to Holyrood, then drive west on the Conception Bay Highway (Route 60) for approximately 500 metres to the beach.
AMENITIES: Wheelchair-accessible boardwalk, picnic area, benches.
NEARBY: George Cove Mountain Trail (1 kilometre), Holy Cross Swim Park (1.5 kilometres), Murray's Peak Hiking Trail (5 kilometres), The Tide (8 kilometres).

AVALON PENINSULA & ISTHMUS OF AVALON

64 Manuels Beach

Manuels Beach is one of a string of cobble beaches found along the coastline of Conception Bay South; similar beaches are at Chamberlains, Lance Cove, and Long Pond, among other locations. Manuels Beach lies at the north end of the Ocean Trail East along the Manuels River, internationally recognized for its trilobite fossils.

The trail begins at the Manuels River Interpretation Centre on Route 60 but can also be accessed from the parking lot on the opposite side of the highway. It passes first alongside the cascades at Little Canyon and then follows the river for approximately 2 kilometres to Bubble Pond and the beach. Cross the bridge about 400 metres into the hike to stay on the east side of the river; the beach cannot be accessed from the western section of the trail. The trail is flat and well groomed, and dogs are welcome on leash.

The beach can also be accessed more directly from the residential neighbourhood of Worsley Park. A clubhouse near the beach can be rented for special events but is not open to the public. Parking is permitted in the paved lot by the clubhouse.

Manuels Beach is ideal for watching the sun set over Kelly's Island a few kilometres offshore. According to local tradition, the uninhabited island is named after a pirate who buried treasure there in the 17th century. Do not bother with a treasure hunt, though, as tradition also holds that it was recovered by unknown visitors in 1920.

COORDINATES: 47.533338, -52.954553 (parking lot); 47.534423, -52.955794 (beach).
DIRECTIONS: To access the beach from Worsley Park, get onto the Conception Bay Highway (Route 60) and take Chamberlains Road and Worsley Drive to Worsley Park.
AMENITIES: Benches along the trail.
NEARBY: Chamberlains Park and Trail (2 kilometres), Topsail Beach (4 kilometres), Octagon Pond Trail (8 kilometres).

AVALON PENINSULA & ISTHMUS OF AVALON

65 Topsail Beach

In the 1800s, the community of Topsail, less than 30 kilometres from St. John's, was a choice destination for vacationers looking to escape the city. These days, most St. John's residents travel farther afield for vacations, but Topsail Beach remains a popular day-use area.

The long, cobble beach is in Topsail Beach Rotary Park, which also has a playground, gazebo, amphitheatre, benches, and picnic tables. A large wheelchair-accessible area with picnic tables overlooks the beach. Public bathrooms are in a building next to the playground, and a small canteen sometimes operates in the summer. Campfires are permitted on the beach, with metal firepits provided.

Although the water is quite cold, some hardy souls venture in. Others prefer to sit on the beach and enjoy the view. Bell Island, Little Bell Island, and Kelly's Island are all visible from the beach, as is the ferry that runs between Bell Island and Portugal

Cove. A freshwater pond opposite the beach offers relatively warmer water for swimming.

The East Coast Trail begins at Topsail Beach just east of the parking lot. A steep climb up a side trail will also take you up to Topsail Bluff for a panoramic view of Conception Bay. Alternatively, you can reach the viewpoint from the top of Summit Drive. Scramble over the boulders at the back of the gravel parking area and take the 200-metre walking trail through the woods to the bluff.

COORDINATES: 47.542988, -52.920382 (beach); 47.543994, -52.911100 (trail to Topsail Bluff from Summit Drive).

DIRECTIONS: From Conception Bay Highway (Route 60), turn onto Topsail Beach Road and follow the road to the large, circular parking lot at the end.

AMENITIES: Bathrooms, picnic tables, beaches, gazebo, firepits.

NEARBY: Chamberlains Park and Trail (3 kilometres), Manuels River Trail (4 kilometres), Manuels Beach (5 kilometres), Octagon Pond Trail (5 kilometres).

AVALON PENINSULA & ISTHMUS OF AVALON

66 Beachy Cove

In a basin bounded on three sides by steep hills, this small beach feels secluded, despite being just off the main road through Portugal Cove. A waterfall cascades down the hill at the back of the cove. To get a closer view of the falls, wade up the shallow brook that runs past clusters of wildflowers before emptying into the ocean.

The beach offers a view of Bell Island. Sit and watch the ferries on their runs between the island and Portugal Cove, take a dip, or wait for twilight and see the sun set over Conception Bay.

At the south side of the cove, on the hill above the beach, a wooden staircase disappears into the forest. This is the Long Shore Path, a 17.2-kilometre hiking trail (part of the East Coast Trail) that extends from Topsail Beach to a site near the ferry terminal in Portugal Cove. Climb the stairs for another view of Conception Bay.

COORDINATES: 47.616442, -52.869944 (path entrance); 47.617374, -52.870516 (beach).
DIRECTIONS: Head west on Beachy Cove Road in Portugal Cove. Approximately 1.5 kilometres past Ferry Terminal Road is a low stone wall on the right. A short distance past the wall is a small gravel parking area, and just beyond that, a white boulder marks the 100-metre path to the beach.
AMENITIES: Picnic tables.
NEARBY: Ferry to Bell Island (2 kilometres), Picco's Ridge Hiking Trail (3 kilometres), St. Philip's Beach (5 kilometres), Torbay Beach (13 kilometres), Topsail Beach (15 kilometres).

AVALON PENINSULA & ISTHMUS OF AVALON

67 Lance Cove

Lance Cove Beach is unusual on Bell Island for its ease of access. While most beaches on the island lie below sheer cliffs, Lance Cove Beach is in a valley that slopes gently to sea level. It's not surprising that this was one of the earliest places on Bell Island to be settled.

The road down to the beach is approximately 7 kilometres southwest of the ferry terminal, off O'Neal's Hill Road. On the left as you approach the beach is the Seaman's Memorial, erected by the Royal Canadian Legion in 1995. The memorial honours sailors who lost their lives in U-boat attacks on ships anchored off Lance Cove during World War II.

Lance Cove is not a swimming beach, but you can sit and enjoy the view of Conception Bay or walk the beach and marvel at the large rectangular beach rocks. Unlike the rounded cobbles found on most Newfoundland beaches, these rocks were not deposited by glaciers but were slabs that broke off cliffs in the area and became worn over time by wave action.

COORDINATES: 47.60037, -52.97746.

DIRECTIONS: On Bell Island, head southwest on Lance Cove Road for approximately 7 kilometres until you reach an intersection with Reeses Hill Road on the right and O'Neal's Hill Road on the left. Make a sharp left onto O'Neal's Hill Road then a quick right onto Lance Cove Beach Road. Follow this road down to the beach. Park in the gravel lot in front of the beach.

AMENITIES: Picnic tables, gazebo.

NEARBY: Bell Island Community Museum and Mine Tour (7 kilometres), Bell Island Lighthouse (9 kilometres), Grebe's Nest (9 kilometres).

AVALON PENINSULA & ISTHMUS OF AVALON

68 Grebe's Nest

Grebe's Nest on Bell Island is surrounded on three sides by sheer cliff faces. The only way to access the beach is through a 75-metre-long tunnel blasted through the rock in 1968 by local fishers because landing at neighbouring Big Cove was too dangerous. Proper footwear and a flashlight are advised.

Upon emerging into Grebe's Nest, you are rewarded with views of the striated 30-metre-high cliffs and of Conception Bay North. Look for trace fossils in the rocks. Bell Island is famous for fossilized tracks, trails, and burrows created by soft-bodied animals as they moved through the sediment 450 million years ago.

En route to Grebe's Nest, at Big Cove, is a rock formation known as Shoe Rock. Walk out onto the flat section for a closer look at the sandstone and shale layers characteristic of cliffs around Bell Island. At the base of the stack, a band of red ironstone is a reminder of Bell Island's iron ore mining history.

COORDINATES: 47.641443, -52.978170 (path to Big Cove); 47.640105, -52.979236 (Grebe's Nest).

DIRECTIONS: On Bell Island, drive to the end of the pavement on Carter's Avenue, on the north side of the island. Find space to park and walk the rest of the way along the rough dirt road, about 0.5 kilometres. Descend the path to Big Cove and take the tunnel to Grebe's Nest.

AMENITIES: None.

NEARBY: Bell Island Community Museum and Mine Tour (3 kilometres), Bell Island Lighthouse (6 kilometres), Lance Cove Beach and Seaman's Memorial (9 kilometres).

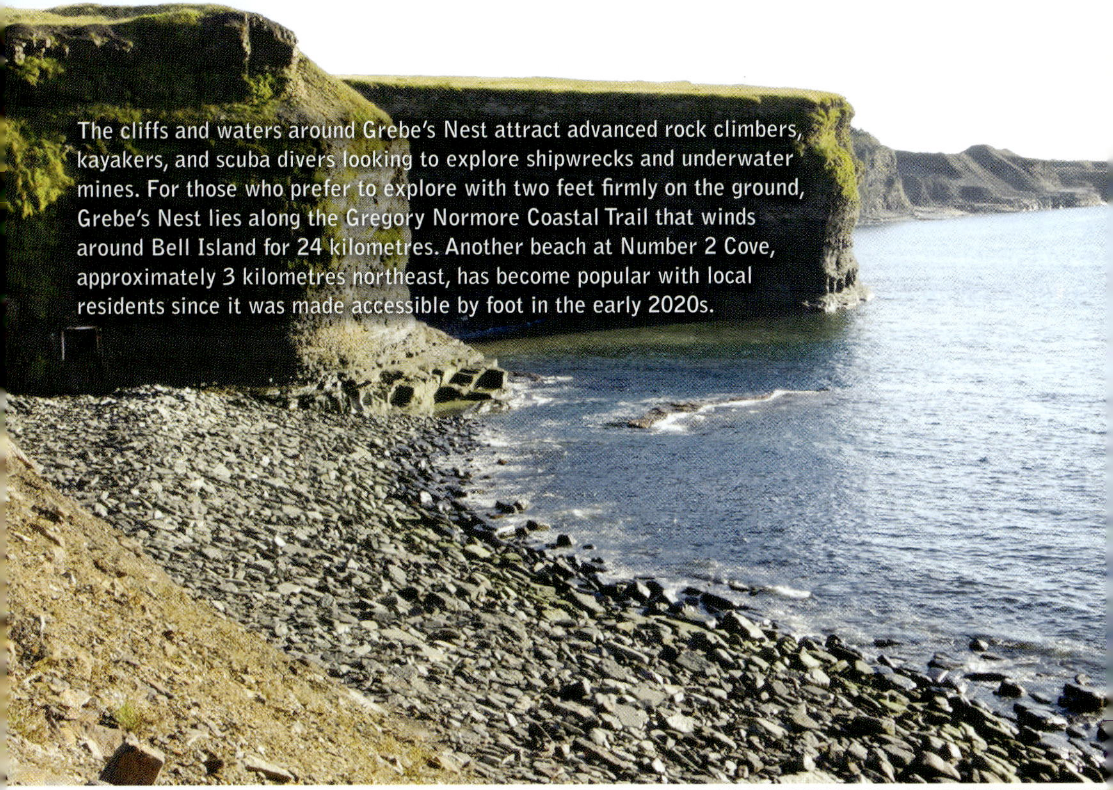

The cliffs and waters around Grebe's Nest attract advanced rock climbers, kayakers, and scuba divers looking to explore shipwrecks and underwater mines. For those who prefer to explore with two feet firmly on the ground, Grebe's Nest lies along the Gregory Normore Coastal Trail that winds around Bell Island for 24 kilometres. Another beach at Number 2 Cove, approximately 3 kilometres northeast, has become popular with local residents since it was made accessible by foot in the early 2020s.

AVALON PENINSULA & ISTHMUS OF AVALON

69 Torbay Beach

In the town of Torbay, the ocean washes ashore at Torbay Bight, a cove surrounded by steep, grass-covered slopes dotted with trees and houses. In the 1700s, the cobble beach was the site of a battery erected partly in response to invasions by the French army, and in 1762, British troops landed at the beach on their way to recapture St. John's after it was seized by the French. A monument uphill from the beach recounts the event.

Torbay Beach is a peaceful spot to enjoy a dose of fresh ocean air and scenery. Providing a picturesque backdrop to the beach is a small nature conservation area with a waterfall rushing down into a lush green valley. Take the short walk up the hill along the Woodfines Falls Trail to view a portion of the falls from above. A little farther up the trail, a bridge crosses over the brook that feeds the falls. Although the falls are not visible from this vantage point, it does afford a view of the ocean.

Father Troy's Trail, a section of the East Coast Trail, also runs through the area. The 8.7-kilometre trail begins up the hill from the beach on the south side of Torbay Bight. It descends and crosses the beach, then climbs again on the north side of the Bight for a panoramic view of the beach and the town.

COORDINATES: 47.659621, -52.730660.

DIRECTIONS: From Torbay Road (Route 20), turn onto Lower Street and continue for about 430 metres to The Battery. Park in the small gravel parking area or continue to the right for another 100 metres to a paved parking area next to the beach.

AMENITIES: Benches.

NEARBY: Torbay Museum (1 kilometre), Middle Cove Beach (5 kilometres), Outer Cove Beach (6 kilometres).

AVALON PENINSULA & ISTHMUS OF AVALON

70 Middle Cove

Summer or winter, this sand and pebble beach 15 minutes outside St. John's always has something to offer. In warm weather, residents and visitors come to sunbathe, picnic, and enjoy the scenery. A panoramic view of the beach and ocean can also be enjoyed from Middle Cove Lookout, about 500 metres east on Marine Drive. After dark, the beach lights up as people gather around campfires with family and friends.

Middle Cove is one of the most popular beaches on the Avalon Peninsula during the annual caplin roll, when people descend on the beach in large numbers with nets and buckets. Whales may also be seen during this time as they come to feed on the caplin.

In winter, a wall of gigantic icicles often forms on the cliffs surrounding the beach. This natural wonder attracts sightseers and photographers, but it must be enjoyed from a distance as the ice is unstable and falling chunks can cause serious injury.

Extreme caution should also be exercised when swimming at Middle Cove, as the waves can be strong and unpredictable.

Silver Mine Head Path, a part of the East Coast Trail, begins at the north end of the beach and follows the coastline for approximately 2.5 kilometres to Motion Drive in Torbay. The hike is rated as easy.

COORDINATES: 47.650343, -52.696393.

DIRECTIONS: Middle Cove Beach is just off Marine Drive (Route 30), 250 metres west of Outer Cove Road. A paved lot offers parking adjacent to the beach, including one handicapped-accessible spot.

AMENITIES: Picnic tables.

NEARBY: Outer Cove Beach (2 kilometres), Museum of Logy Bay-Middle Cove-Outer Cove (3 kilometres), Torbay Beach (5 kilometres).

AVALON PENINSULA & ISTHMUS OF AVALON

71 Outer Cove

Outer Cove Beach is 2 kilometres west of Middle Cove Beach, on the opposite side of a triangular-shaped headland. It attracts fewer visitors than Middle Cove Beach as it is smaller and rockier, and parking is limited. This does, however, make it a relatively quiet place to have a campfire, fish, or enjoy the fresh air and scenic views.

In 1980, Terry Fox filled a bottle with Atlantic seawater at Outer Cove Beach before beginning his cross-country run for cancer research, with the intention of ultimately emptying the bottle into the Pacific Ocean. Fox's story is recounted on a Parks Canada interpretive sign at the Outer Cove Lookout on Marine Drive, 0.5 kilometres up the hill from the beach. A mural depicting him is painted on the wall of the underpass leading to the beach, and another mural adorns the opposite wall of the underpass.

COORDINATES: 47.650398, -52.682740 (path to beach from Lower Road); 47.651048, -52.682754 (beach).

DIRECTIONS: In the town of Logy Bay-Middle Cove-Outer Cove, follow Lower Road north almost to the end where it meets Marine Drive. Approximately 30 metres before Marine Drive is a small gravel clearing. Park there but do not block the gate. Walk down the hill and through the underpass to the beach.

AMENITIES: None.

NEARBY: Cobbler Path Hiking Trail (1 kilometre), Middle Cove Beach (2 kilometres), Torbay Beach (5 kilometres).

AVALON PENINSULA & ISTHMUS OF AVALON

72 Ragged Beach

Ragged Beach is the first of several beaches along Beaches Path, a 7-kilometre hiking trail that extends south from the town of Witless Bay to Mobile. This is one of the most accessible stretches of pristine, untouched coastline in Eastern Newfoundland, and the terrain along the trail is generally flat and easy to navigate. The trail follows the route of an old walking path that has existed for generations; locals used the area to hunt, tend gardens, pick berries, and gather mussels. Look for the trailhead on the forested bank above the beach.

The beach can be enjoyed in all seasons for its rugged beauty and assortment of pebbles and boulders of many shapes, sizes, and colours. Caplin come to the area in early summer but do not wash ashore, because of the roughness of the shoreline; however, the whales that arrive to feed on the caplin can often be spotted.

Just offshore is Witless Bay Ecological Reserve, a collection of four islands that are home to the largest Atlantic puffin colony in North America. These birds, which use natural light sources to navigate, rely on Ragged Beach because it is a dark coastline free of disruptive artificial light sources. Efforts have been made to protect the area from development, and the view of the stars on a clear night is outstanding.

COORDINATES: 47.262353, -52.811459.

DIRECTIONS: From Route 10 in Witless Bay, turn onto Gallows Cove Road and follow it 2 kilometres to the end (the last 100 metres is unpaved). Park in the gravel clearing adjacent to the beach.

AMENITIES: None.

NEARBY: Mickeleen's Path (5 kilometres); Mobile Beach (5 kilometres); boat tours in Witless Bay (2 kilometres), Mobile (5 kilometres), and Bay Bulls (8 kilometres).

AVALON PENINSULA & ISTHMUS OF AVALON

73 Mobile Beach

Located in the town of Mobile just off Route 10, Mobile Beach is a mixture of rocks of varying sizes, from rounded pebbles to angular boulders to outcroppings of rippled shale. Take a leisurely walk on the beach to search for driftwood, or watch the seabirds resting on bright green, algae-covered rocks at the water's edge. Adding to the sensory experience is the crunch of dried seaweed underfoot and the sound of the Mobile River as it empties into the ocean at the south end of the beach.

For those interested in a longer walk, the southern trailhead for Beaches Path, part of the East Coast Trail, begins at the north end of the beach. Hugging the coastline for 7 kilometres to Witless Bay, it includes several other rocky beaches along the way, including Ragged Beach at the end of the trail. Throughout the summer, get a closer look at whales and puffins by taking one of the boat tours available in Mobile and surrounding communities.

COORDINATES: 47.248543, -52.840780.

DIRECTIONS: From Route 10, turn onto Riverhead Road and park in the high school parking lot. Cross the highway and follow the gravel path that runs past the white house to the beach. It looks like a private driveway but is open to the public.

AMENITIES: None.

NEARBY: Ragged Beach (5 kilometres), Tors Cove Beach (5 kilometres), La Manche Provincial Park (16 kilometres).

Most people find the water too cold for swimming at Mobile Beach. The Whale House Guesthouse in Mobile has an excellent blog entry directing readers to an outdoor pool, swimming holes, and freshwater beaches in the area. Google "Whale House secret beaches."

AVALON PENINSULA & ISTHMUS OF AVALON

74 Tors Cove Beach

Tors Cove Beach (sometimes called Lower Beach) is at the southern end of Tinkers Point Path, a 5-kilometre section of the East Coast Trail that runs between Mobile and Tors Cove. For the quickest and easiest access to the beach, start from the trailhead on Cove Road in Tors Cove and follow the path a few hundred metres down to the coast.

Just offshore is Fox Island, used by farmers as grazing pasture for sheep throughout the summer. More islands are visible farther south, including Great Island and Pee Pee Island, which constitute the southern edge of the Witless Bay Ecological Reserve. Puffins and other birds that nest on these islands and feed in the surrounding waters can often be spotted from the beach, but bring binoculars for a close-up view.

On the bluff above the beach is Cribbies Meadow, a popular picnic spot and excellent vantage point for whale watching. From the meadow, the Tinkers Point Trail passes alongside two colourful heritage homes featured in postcards and tourism commercials.

To explore more rocky beaches, continue along the trail to Beachy Cove, Kearney's Beach, and Deep Cove. Gentle and easy to navigate, the trail is suitable for families and has almost continuous coastal views. Watch for seals lounging on the rocks.

COORDINATES: 47.214516, -52.845492 (trailhead); 47.213131, -52.842000 (beach).
DIRECTIONS: From Route 10 in Tors Cove, turn onto Cove Road and drive about 500 metres to a gravel parking lot on the left (prior site of the Sacred Heart Catholic Church). Follow the Tinkers Point Path, across from the parking lot, a few hundred metres to the beach.
AMENITIES: Picnic tables.
NEARBY: Tors Cove Pond swimming area (2 kilometres), Mobile Beach (5 kilometres), Ragged Beach (9 kilometres), La Manche Provincial Park (13 kilometres).

AVALON PENINSULA & ISTHMUS OF AVALON

75 Ferryland Beach

Ferryland Beach has both scenic beauty and historical significance. It lies at the site of one of the earliest permanent English colonies in Newfoundland: The Colony of Avalon, established in 1621. Archaeological excavations have uncovered remarkably well-preserved remains of buildings, a cobblestone road, and thousands of artifacts, many of which can be viewed at the Visitor Centre across the parking lot from the beach.

The beach is on the south side of the isthmus to "The Downs," the peninsula that extends into Ferryland Harbour. It offers a superb view of The Downs, including Ferryland Head at the eastern end of the peninsula. From the beach, it's an easy 1-kilometre walk to the lighthouse, a popular place to picnic while scanning the water for whales. (A company called Lighthouse Picnics will prepare a meal for you on the lighthouse grounds; spaces fill up quickly, so reserve well in advance.)

In addition to the main beach, smaller beaches line other sections of coastline

along the peninsula, including on the north side of the isthmus. Overlooking that beach is an 8-foot-tall monument to Ron Hynes, one of Newfoundland and Labrador's most revered musical artists. Hynes, who grew up in Ferryland, died in 2015 and was inducted into the Canadian Songwriters Hall of Fame in 2020.

COORDINATES: 47.022695, -52.883303.
DIRECTIONS: Take Route 10 to Pool Road in Ferryland and park at the Colony of Avalon Visitor Centre. Access the beach at the east end of the parking lot.
AMENITIES: Bathrooms, gift shop, restaurant.
NEARBY: Caplin Bay Path (<1 kilometre), Sounding Hills Path (<1 kilometre), Cape Broyle Head Path (11 kilometres).

AVALON PENINSULA & ISTHMUS OF AVALON

76 Cappahayden Beach

Cappahayden Beach is on a stretch of coastline often referred to as the "Graveyard of the Atlantic," on account of the number of shipwrecks that have occurred there. Most famous is the sinking of the *Florizel* on the morning of February 24, 1918.

Due to a combination of poor weather and human error, the luxury passenger liner with 138 people on board ran full speed into a reef at Horn Head Point, just south of Cappahayden. Ninety-four people perished, including a 3-year-old girl named Betty Munn, to whom the Peter Pan statue in Bowring Park in St. John's is dedicated. A book by Newfoundland and Labrador author Cassie Brown, *A Winter's Tale*, recounts the disaster.

On a hill overlooking the beach, a memorial remembers the tragedy and pays homage to those who helped rescue the survivors. A full list of victims is displayed, along with a piece of the wreckage. More debris lies along the banks near Horn Head,

but most of it has been reclaimed by the earth or removed by visitors to the site.

COORDINATES: 46.860666, -52.945428 (parking and trailhead); 46.860823, -52.943563 (beach).

DIRECTIONS: From Route 10 in Cappahayden, take Old Southern Shore Road a short distance to the *Florizel* site parking area, then follow the short trail to the memorial. A rough footpath leads down to the beach.

AMENITIES: Bench at memorial.

NEARBY: Island Meadow Hiking Path (<1 kilometre), Bear Cove Point Path (12 kilometres), Chance Cove Provincial Park (13 kilometres), *Ilex* shipwreck (18 kilometres).

To learn more about shipwrecks along this coastline, visit Bear Cove Lookout, approximately 2 kilometres north of the *Florizel* site on Route 10. The site includes an interpretive sign, picnic table, and a roadside beach.

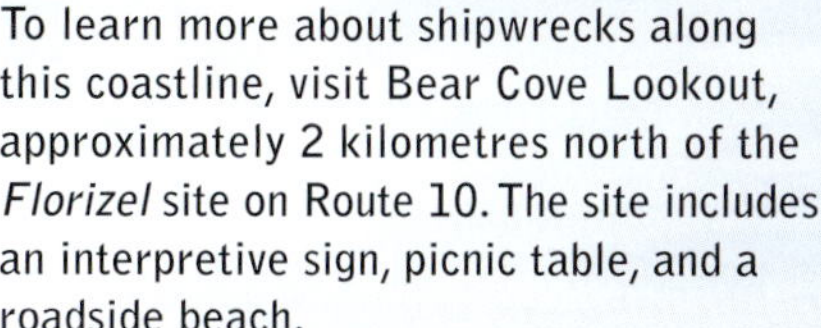

77 Portugal Cove South

On the southeastern tip of the Avalon Peninsula, along a 17-kilometre stretch of coastline from Portugal Cove South to Cape Race, is Mistaken Point Ecological Reserve, home to the oldest known multi-cellular fossils on earth. Driving through the reserve is permitted, but accessing the fossil site requires a guided tour, arranged through the Edge of Avalon Interpretive Centre in Portugal Cove South.

Visitors may also want to explore the lovely beaches that lie along the route through the reserve. At the beginning of the road to Cape Race in Portugal Cove South, a long cobble beach curves around the cove. Relax on a bench and enjoy the view before heading into the reserve.

Drive about 5 kilometres south along the route to reach picturesque Drook Cove, backed by rolling hills and a handful of quaint summer cottages. Visible along the south side of the cove are the huge, overlapping slabs of rock that form part of the fossil-rich Drook Formation.

Nine kilometres past Drook Cove—and just down the hill from the Ranger Station—is Long Beach. The guided tours of Mistaken Point depart from the Ranger Station, making the beach a convenient and scenic place to picnic before or after a tour. From Long Beach, it's another 6 kilometres to Cape Race Lighthouse, famous for receiving the *Titanic*'s first distress call.

COORDINATES: 46.711458, -53.261623 (Portugal Cove South Beach); 46.671678, -53.242427 (Drook Cove); 46.639964, -53.137800 (Long Beach).

DIRECTIONS: From Route 10 in Portugal Cove South, turn onto Harbour Road/Cape Race Road. Continue for 5 kilometres to Drook Cove, and another 9 kilometres to Long Beach. Much of the road is unpaved but well maintained.

AMENITIES: Benches at Portugal Cove South Beach, picnic tables at Long Beach, bathrooms at both the Interpretive Centre and Ranger Station.

NEARBY*: Biscay Bay Beach (5 kilometres), Trepassey Beach (13 kilometres), Chance Cove Provincial Park (19 kilometres).

*Distances calculated from Portugal Cove South Beach.

Photo © Mistaken Point Ambassadors Inc.

AVALON PENINSULA & ISTHMUS OF AVALON

78 Biscay Bay

Biscay Bay is on the southeast coast of the Avalon Peninsula, about midway between the towns of Trepassey and Portugal Cove South. With its soft, fine sand, Biscay Bay Beach is a favourite spot for people from the area to relax, swim, and even surf when the waves are high. According to local residents, it's also an excellent place to search for sand dollars and other treasures at low tide.

The barachois beach stretches across the bottom of the 4-kilometre-long, rectangular-shaped bay, separating the sea water from Biscay Bay Pond. Route 10 runs alongside the beach across the sandbar, making the beach easy to access while touring the Irish Loop.

Historically, Biscay Bay was known for its rich salmon resources, and the salmon fishery employed many residents of the area. Most residents now commute to larger centres for work, but people still come to fish recreationally for salmon in the Biscay Bay River north of the beach.

The Biscay Bay Trail follows the licensed salmon river into the Avalon Wilderness Reserve for 13 kilometres. The trail is for hikers only; off-road vehicles are not permitted.

COORDINATES: 46.743331, -53.288074.

DIRECTIONS: From Route 10 in Biscay Bay, take the gravel road that runs alongside the west end of the beach, called "Old Road," and park on the side of the road. Alternatively, pull in off Route 10 at the eastern end of the beach, in front of Biscay Bay Gut.

AMENITIES: None.

NEARBY: Mistaken Point Ecological Reserve (8 kilometres), Drook Cove (11 kilometres), Powles Head Lighthouse (13 kilometres).

AVALON PENINSULA & ISTHMUS OF AVALON

79 St. Shott's Beach

On the tip of the landmass separating Trepassey Bay from St. Mary's Bay, St. Shott's is the southernmost town in Newfoundland and Labrador. It's a 13-kilometre detour off the Irish Loop, but well worth the drive to view the sunset from the southwesterly facing sand and cobble beach. A grassy bank above the beach is the perfect vantage point.

The view looking southeastward is equally impressive, as the sea crashes against a cluster of angular boulders. This part of the Avalon Peninsula is one of the foggiest places on the island, so check the forecast before visiting to make the most of the scenery.

With fewer than 70 residents, St. Shott's has limited amenities; ensure that you have enough gas, food, and other necessities for the return trip. Since 2022, a bed-and-breakfast called the Keeper's Kitchen has been attracting visitors to the tiny town with gourmet meals, house concerts, and guided tours of the area; reservations are required.

COORDINATES: 46.707885, -53.474589 (turnoff onto St. Shott's Road from Route 10); 46.632899, -53.590210 (beach).

DIRECTIONS: From Route 10, take St. Shott's Road into St. Shott's and turn right onto Church Road. Park at Our Lady of Fatima Catholic Church and walk down the hill to the beach, about 150 metres.

AMENITIES: None.

NEARBY: St. Shott's Light Station at Eastern Head (2 kilometres), Cape Pine Lighthouse (18 kilometres).

A few kilometres east of St. Shott's stands the oldest cast-iron lighthouse in Canada. The Cape Pine Lighthouse was erected in 1851 in response to numerous shipwrecks that occurred along the southeast coast of the Avalon Peninsula. From Cape Pine, a hiking trail leads to another beautiful beach at Arnold's Cove. Ask the locals for directions or inquire at the Keeper's Kitchen B&B.

AVALON PENINSULA & ISTHMUS OF AVALON

80 St. Vincent's Beach

St. Vincent's Beach provides an opportunity to view humpback whales up close without boarding a boat, owing to a sharp drop-off just metres from the shoreline. Around late June to early July, the giant creatures come to feed on caplin, to the delight of spectators and photographers gathered on the coarse grey sand and pebbles.

Whales are more likely to be seen at the eastern end of the beach, near the main parking area and bridge. A wheelchair-accessible platform off the parking lot offers a view of the beach and water. To find out if the whales are in the area, look on the St. Vincent's-St. Stephens-Peter's River Facebook page, as members report sightings.

At 5 kilometres in length, St. Vincent's Beach is an excellent place for a long walk to enjoy the ocean air and scenery. Northern gannets also come to St. Vincent's to feed on caplin, and they can often be seen dramatically plunge-diving into the water at high speed. Be sure to enjoy the sights from the shore; the drop-off and strong currents make the beach far too dangerous for swimming. Also remember to bring warm clothes, as it can get quite chilly, even in the summer.

COORDINATES: 46.789364, -53.638470.

DIRECTIONS: From the TCH, head south on Salmonier Line (Route 90) for approximately 80 kilometres. As you reach the end of Holyrood Pond, the road curves left and continues along the beach for another 1.5 kilometres to the parking area on the right.

AMENITIES: Picnic tables in parking area, bathrooms in Holyrood Pond Interpretation Centre across the road.

NEARBY: St. Mary's Battery Park (18 kilometres), Gulch Beach (19 kilometres).

AVALON PENINSULA & ISTHMUS OF AVALON

81 Gulch Beach

Gulch Beach, in Point La Haye, is a 1-kilometre-long gravel bar separating Point La Haye Pond from St. Mary's Bay. From the pond, the beach is accessed via a wooden walkway and wheelchair-accessible ramp that winds through shrubs and clusters of wildflowers. Two picnic tables are situated along the walkway and a signboard recounts the history of the area.

At the end of the ramp, either turn left onto the beach, or turn right to follow a footpath up the hill to a lookout on the grassy plateau. Beyond the lookout, the path continues along the coast, with occasional sections of boardwalk through marshy areas. Signs along the path tell stories of lives lost at sea. You may also encounter irises blooming alongside the path, or ripe blueberries in late summer. The path continues north for approximately 4 kilometres to Battery Park in the town of St. Mary's.

Gulch Beach is not suitable for swimming due to the cold and often rough water, but many visitors swim in Point La Haye Pond. Near the pond are change rooms, outhouses, a large picnic area, and parking for recreational vehicles. The park hosts community events, such as the annual Gulch Beach Festival and Car Show. Information about this and other events can be found on the Gulch Days Facebook page.

COORDINATES: 46.902314, -53.611751.

DIRECTIONS: From Salmonier Line (Route 90), turn onto Gulch Road. Follow this road to the park and beach, approximately 2 kilometres. Park in the unpaved area near the beach.

AMENITIES: Outhouses, change rooms, picnic area.

NEARBY: St. Mary's First Falls Walking Trail (4 kilometres), St. Vincent's Beach (18 kilometres).

197

AVALON PENINSULA & ISTHMUS OF AVALON

82 Point Lance Sands

At the southwestern tip of the Avalon Peninsula, and 11 kilometres off the Cape Shore highway, Point Lance is remote. The community is small with few amenities, but the beach is one of just a handful of sandy beaches on the Avalon, making it a hidden gem.

With its fine sand and long, rolling waves, the beach is an attractive destination for people interested in swimming, boating, and surfing. Remember to use caution when engaging in water activities at unsupervised beaches. For children, a safer place to splash in the water is about halfway down the beach, where Conway's Brook pools and then drains into the ocean. Look for the small yellow bridge over the brook, which can also be accessed via an ATV trail that runs through the meadow above the beach.

At the western end of the beach, a rough gravel road winds up and around the point for approximately 1.5 kilometres. Named Tilt Road, the route offers scenic views and leads to a site where men once spent summers in cabins ("tilts") to be closer to the fishing grounds. Geology enthusiasts will appreciate the outcrop of diabase—rare in this region—about 200 metres up the hill.

COORDINATES: 46.810106, -54.087177.
DIRECTIONS: Approximately 4.5 kilometres west of the town of Branch, follow the highway sign toward Point Lance (the turnoff is at 46.881620, -54.008029). Drive for approximately 11 kilometres, passing through the community of Point Lance, and park in the small unpaved lot at the western end of the beach.
AMENITIES: None.
NEARBY: Cape St. Mary's Ecological Reserve (33 kilometres).

In 2022, Point Lance experienced an unusually large number of Portuguese men-of-war washing up on the beach. Keep your distance from these organisms as they deliver painful and sometimes dangerous stings.

Photo © Robert Ryan

AVALON PENINSULA & ISTHMUS OF AVALON

83 Gooseberry Cove

Gooseberry Cove lies in a lush river valley on the eastern shore of Placentia Bay, less than 30 kilometres southwest of the town of Placentia. Once the site of a small farming and fishing community, it was designated a public beach after the last residents moved away in the 1950s. Today, it operates as a provincial park. Overnight camping, off-road vehicles, and campfires are not permitted on the beach. Pets must be kept on leash.

The sandy beach is tucked away in a protected cove at the end of a narrow laneway lined with wild rose bushes. It can be difficult to spot, especially when heading south. Watch for the cottages and a small gravel parking area just down the hill from the sign for Gooseberry Cove.

While a few cottages cluster around the beach, most visitors come to Gooseberry Cove as day users to picnic on the grassy banks, wade into the water, or walk barefoot in the soft sand. Waves can be high, making swimming and other water activities difficult.

COORDINATES: 47.071036, -54.093215.

DIRECTIONS: From the town of Placentia, follow Route 100 south for approximately 27 kilometres. After the sign for Gooseberry Cove, descend the hill and pull into the small gravel area on the right. Park and walk down the laneway to the beach, about 150 metres.

AMENITIES: None.

NEARBY: Great Beach in Placentia (27 kilometres), Castle Hill Historic Site (30 kilometres), Cape St. Mary's Ecological Reserve (37 kilometres).

Facing almost due west, Gooseberry Cove is the perfect location to watch the sun go down. Many photographers have used the cove as a stunning backdrop. Google "Seas Change by Youngtree and the Blooms" to view a video shot on the beach by local musical artists.

AVALON PENINSULA & ISTHMUS OF AVALON

84 Great Beach

Great Beach borders the western edge of the town of Placentia. Much of the town is built on what was once a sprawling beach; if you were to dig below the pavement and lawns, you would find thousands of the same cobblestones that cover Great Beach.

A 1.4-kilometre boardwalk runs the length of the beach and is built atop a breakwater that protects the sea-level town from flooding. The boardwalk is wheelchair accessible on both ends and can be accessed by staircases at several points along Beach Road. As you stroll the boardwalk, take in the scent of the immense wild rose bushes proliferating nearby. The Sir Ambrose Shea Bridge, the only vertical lift bridge in the province, is visible in the distance.

In addition to its natural beauty, Great Beach played an important role in the economy of the area. Before houses and streets claimed the space, the wide, cobble beach was ideal for curing cod, and the Basque operated a thriving seasonal fishery there as early as the 16th century. Throughout the 17th and early 18th centuries, French and British armies fought over control of the area until the Treaty of Utrecht ceded control to the British. For more history, as well as a panoramic view of the beach, visit Castle Hill National Historic Site.

COORDINATES: 47.247018, -53.964825.
DIRECTIONS: From the TCH, take Route 100 to Placentia, turning left in Ferndale and then left again in Jerseyside. Cross the bridge and turn right onto Beach Road. Park in the small area at the start of the boardwalk, or continue on Beach Road and park in the larger lot at the opposite end of the boardwalk.
AMENITIES: Boardwalk, gazebo, benches.
NEARBY: O'Reilly House Museum (<1 kilometre), Castle Hill Historic Site (3 kilometres), First Beach (5 kilometres), Argentia ferry to Nova Scotia (8 kilometres).

AVALON PENINSULA & ISTHMUS OF AVALON

Resources

Trail guides

AllTrails: www.alltrails.com

East Coast Trail: eastcoasttrail.com

Outer Bay of Islands Enhancement Committee: www.obiec.ca

Trailforks: www.trailforks.com

Wikiloc.com—Trails guide: www.wikiloc.com

Databases and encyclopedias

Canadian Register of Historic Places (CRHP): www.historicplaces.ca

eBird Canada: ebird.org/canada

Heritage Foundation of Newfoundland and Labrador: heritagenl.ca

Iceberg Finder: icebergfinder.com

Parks, government, & association sites

Canadian Parks and Wilderness Society: Newfoundland and Labrador Chapter: cpawsnl.org

Museum Association of Newfoundland and Labrador: museumsnl.ca

Nature Conservancy Canada: Newfoundland and Labrador: www.natureconservancy.ca/en/where-we-work/newfoundland-and-labrador

Newfoundland and Labrador Heritage Website: www.heritage.nf.ca

Newfoundland and Labrador Tourism: www.newfoundlandlabrador.com

Parks Canada: parks.canada.ca

Parks Division Newfoundland and Labrador: www.parksnl.ca

Stewardship Association of Municipalities Inc (SAM): www.samnl.org

Blogs and personal websites

East Waters: www.eastwaters.com

Encounter Newfoundland: encounternewfoundland.com

Explore with Lora: Newfoundland: www.explorewithlora.com/tag/newfoundland

Hidden Newfoundland: www.hiddennewfoundland.ca

Lighthouse Friends: www.lighthousefriends.com

Rocks of Newfoundland Labrador: rocksnl.com

Whale House Guest House: www.whalehouse.ca/blog

Other titles by Boulder Books

Birds of Newfoundland

Geology of Newfoundland

Hidden Newfoundland

Hikes of Newfoundland

Wildflowers of Newfoundland and Labrador

Index

Acknowledgements

Creating this guide was more fun than work, and I owe that to the many friends and family who accompanied me on my beach-going adventures: Stacy Smith, Bev Quinton, Judy Molyneux, Chava Finkler, Jeanette Pomroy, Julie Sircom, Stefen Gerriets, Tina King, Heather Long, Clint Smith, Robert Bailey, Damian Follett, and Pirate. I am also grateful to Suzanne Johnson, whose hospitality and delicious meals helped sustain me while writing this guide.

Many thanks to those who contributed photos; page numbers are in brackets: Robert Bailey (35, 49), Isaac Blue (134), Martine Blue (132, 133, 134, 135), Delavan Bungay (143), Paula Burt (73), Mark Gray (112), Linden Jesso (34), Owen Keough (109), Logan MacDonald (110), Mistaken Point Ambassadors Inc (189), Alexandra Noseworthy (149), Bev Quinton (23), Robert Ryan (199), Nicole Shea (191), Julie Sircom (27, 37, 38, 48, 49), and Allan Smith (201).

A special thank you to the people I met on the beaches and in the communities I visited, as well as those with whom I connected through community Facebook pages. Taking the time to chat with me and answer my questions was extremely helpful and greatly appreciated.

Finally, I want to thank the Boulder team for the opportunity to work on this guide and for their invaluable support. It is an honour to be among the authors who, through Boulder's series of guidebooks, are helping people discover Newfoundland's finest features.

About the Author

Growing up in Newfoundland and Hawaii, Carla Smith Krachun developed a deep attachment to the ocean. She is especially fascinated with the widely varying coastline around Newfoundland and has spent countless hours exploring the island's beaches. In addition to doing freelance writing and photography, Carla worked as a photographer with the *Evening Telegram* and writer with the *Encyclopedia of Newfoundland and Labrador*. She taught psychology at Memorial University and the University of Saskatchewan. On returning home to Newfoundland from the prairies, she has enjoyed reacquainting herself with the ocean by writing this book, which she hopes will help others discover and enjoy Newfoundland's many amazing beaches.